PRAISE FOR *FIXING WORK*

"*Fixing Work* is a gift for leaders looking for a practical road map to improve employee engagement, productivity, and customer centricity. Read this book—you'll be glad you did."

—**FAISAL HOQUE,** founder of Shadoka and best-selling author of *Lift* and *Everything Connects*

"In the emerging world of hybrid work, enlisting and engaging employees has become more important than ever. Designing jobs that employees love is going to be table stakes. *Fixing Work* will inspire you to take up this challenge with joy and verve."

—**GEOFFREY MOORE,** speaker, advisor, and author of *Crossing the Chasm*

"Creating work for employees to thrive in has never been more important! *Fixing Work* offers a powerful and practical approach to designing jobs that keep your star performers engaged and productive, and your company on the path to success. Beautifully written and thoughtfully researched, this book will help you start creating the work your team will love today."

—**DR. MARSHALL GOLDSMITH,** executive coach and best-selling author of *The Earned Life* and *What Got You Here Won't Get You There*

"It's no secret that organizations are more productive and successful when workers see how their efforts directly affect company results and when they are part of a team empowered to improve the way work is done. Making this happen, however, is not easy, though it's more important today than ever. If you want a compelling story of how to design a joyful, high-performance workplace, *Fixing Work* is the book for you. Authors Henkin and Bertels, longtime experts in the field of work redesign, provide an easy-to-read, dramatic rendition of one manager's journey from overwhelmed supervisor to transformation leader. If that's a path that you, too, want to take, then the first step is to read this book."

—**RON ASHKENAS,** partner emeritus at Schaffer Consulting

"The power of storytelling comes to life in *Fixing Work*, where we gain a front-row seat to what many managers and employees go through every day. Leaders will readily relate to the highs and lows, ambitions and obstacles facing the future of work, where efficiency gains and cost savings intermingle with the quest for talent, productivity, and high employee engagement. *Fixing Work* narrates what to do—and not do—through a delightful read that is as entertaining as it is helpful."

—**LISHA DAVIS,** CEO at Arable Ventures and adjunct professor at Temple University's Fox School of Business

"I've had the pleasure of working with David Henkin for nearly a decade at Vanguard as we helped enable company growth through a people-first culture. Henkin and Bertels have written a must-read primer for anyone focused on employee engagement, motivation, productivity, and customer centricity.

As employees today, we spend most of our waking hours working, but if the pandemic taught us anything, it taught us that life and work can and should be integrated. It taught us the importance of family, friends, and mental health. It also demonstrated, through the Great Resignation, that we all have choices in the types of organizations we decide to be part of.

Fixing Work is a recipe for attracting and retaining the best talent. It's a handbook on what work should be and what today's employees demand—rewarding work filled with mission, purpose, and a true sense of belonging. Winning organizations of tomorrow will embrace the lessons outlined in this book as a catalyst for success.

The days of leaders maximizing shareholder value have waned and given way to enterprises that have noble missions, value client loyalty, and create incredible experiences for their most valued resource—their people. *Fixing Work* is a must-read for every leader struggling to build a thriving team enabled by an amazing employee culture."

—**JOHN T. MARCANTE,** US CIO-in-Residence at Deloitte

"I worked in HR for more than thirty-five years in the United States, Europe, and Asia, starting in an entry-level position and ending my career as the EVP of a Fortune 20 company. This book, simply put, is wonderful. It is a great story with real-life situations. Makes me want to go back to work and hand it out to every manager."

—PAUL KIRINCIC, former executive vice president
of human resources at McKesson

"*Fixing Work* is a great read for any leader interested in making his or her organization both more productive and a better place to work. Henkin and Bertels have captured the secrets of effective work design and made them highly accessible through a story readers will identify with immediately. I often wonder why all workplaces haven't adopted these principles, which have been around since the '80s and have proven time and time again to work. The answer may be that the information hasn't been communicated in an easily digestible form. With *Fixing Work*, there's no excuse for continuing to waste the precious gifts that employees can offer through creating win-win solutions with their employers. The road to improvement couldn't be made clearer."

—WILLIAM PASMORE, professor of practice of social organizational
psychology at Columbia University's Teachers College

"Anyone who has had leadership responsibility in an organization will immediately recognize that David Henkin and Thomas Bertels feel their pain. The authors share real and relatable world wisdom through the vividly portrayed story of people who have 'been there' and 'done that' in the daily struggle for integrity and relevance at work. This book is sorely needed. Read *Fixing Work* to better serve your company, colleagues, and customers with distinction."

—JEFF WESTPHAL, former chairman and CEO
of Vertex and founder of MeaningSphere

"*Fixing Work* is an easy-to-read, engaging story about a fictional company and a manager facing major problems. Henkin and Bertels weave together ideas, suggestions, and proven tactics to help the manager improve motivation and productivity and, in short, show both the manager and the readers how to make work better. Highly recommend this book for its practical and engaging approach."

—KEVIN WHEELER, founder and president of the Future of Talent Institute

"If you've worked in a large company, you know Jerry. The authors have effectively captured what's broken with work environments similar to Consolidated Insurance. They masterfully introduce us to employees who work to implement well-intended but often temporary fixes. Instead of focusing on the symptoms, much like anesthesia numbs pain, the authors guide us along a pathway that helps companies redefine what work should be for their teams—thereby eliminating the need for employers to create pain-management programs to sedate what's broken—and allows them to turn their full attention to how work can be successfully executed."

—**ERIC REISENWITZ,** former president of group protection at Lincoln Financial Group

"You want a story? You want a business story? Well, here it is. Get a cup of coffee, or a glass of wine, and prepare to learn in ways you've never experienced before. *Fixing Work* is a must-read, but not for the reasons you think: fixing work doesn't have to be grueling; just follow the story. But prepare for a surprise ending."

—**STEPHEN J. ANDRIOLE,** Thomas G. Labrecque Professor at the Villanova School of Business and CEO at TechVestCo

"'People, process, technology.' This has been the business improvement mantra for decades, but usually with process elevated to preeminence and people relegated to the lowest priority. If, instead, you like people and figure they're the true key to business success, David Henkin and Thomas Bertels have authored the book for you. Written as an easy-to-digest business novel, *Fixing Work* illustrates the principles of how improving the employee experience can, in the right hands, make companies more effective and competitive by making how work gets done more rewarding for the people who do it."

—**BOB LEWIS,** president of IT Catalysts

"In today's hybrid work world, engaged employees will define the winners and losers of tomorrow. *Fixing Work* is a must-read for every leader who embraces that reality and needs a plan to make it happen. We all know culture matters. Finally, leaders have a case study that provides the action steps and metrics to enable a differentiated culture. Employees will love it and, more importantly, will deliver better results in it."

—**DAVID DESTEFANO,** president, CEO, and board chair at Vertex

"*Fixing Work* is for anyone who wants to understand the nitty-gritty of the American workplace and how to make work more meaningful, motivating, and productive. Henkin and Bertels's dialogues and stories make the future of work come alive."

—DR. BOB AUBREY, founder of the ASEAN
Human Development Organization

"*Fixing Work* is a corporate page-turner that draws you in immediately by capturing anyone who has ever worked in a business system. The authors highlight the typical dynamics at play that challenge even the most motivated employees to stay engaged. They also spotlight what can happen when one leader is curious enough to seek help from an outside confidant and courageous enough to challenge the way things are—to trust his colleagues to find the answers and to ultimately to get out of their way so they can own their work. The result is an easy-to-read and highly entertaining road map for change that anyone can follow to drive results by unleashing the human potential within their own team or organization."

—GEORGE BREWSTER, founder of Gimbal Systems

"Having worked with Thomas on several projects over the past twenty years, I am well aware of his strategic thinking and organizational design capabilities. The authors' use of storytelling to introduce work design and employee motivation principles results in a thought-provoking yet easy-reading novel. *Fixing Work* is a must-read for any executive seeking to optimize workforce satisfaction while improving productivity."

—DENNIS TRICE, former CEO of Mitsubishi Chemical America

"*Fixing Work* reminds us of our daily challenges and opportunities in our organizations. This a valuable and practical approach to telling a story around challenges we all have encountered. Organizations are seeking ideas on how to win, and it may be right in front of us—improving employee engagement and motivating our employees are connected to productivity and customer satisfaction."

—ROBIN M. ALLEN, senior director of global talent acquisition at Vertex

"What if we thought of work as a product, workers as customers of the product, and managers as designers of the product? The result? More engaged and motivated employees, satisfied customers, and improved productivity. By imbuing work with purpose, autonomy, and feedback; designing work activity for entirety and variety; and ensuring that technology supports that work activity, Jerry Crawford successfully transforms his lackluster group at Consolidated Insurance into a high-performing Mojo Squad. Learn how you can do the same in your organization by reading his compelling transformation story in *Fixing Work*—today!"

—**DR. TONY O'DRISCOLL,** professor of business administration at Duke University and author of *Everyday Superhero*

"*Fixing Work* is the perfect book for helping leaders at all levels drive customer centricity through employee engagement. The book addresses how to manage the complex process of team building, rapid improvement, and maximizing the diverse skills within a typical team. The authors understand the whole system in today's workplace—from the value of executive sponsorship to perfecting processes at the operating level. Their step-by-step analysis is spot-on and a rarity in business books. This is an important business primer at a time when workplace dynamics are screaming out for change."

—**CHRISTOPHER N. DISIPIO,** CEO of Global Benefits Group

"*Fixing Work* offers a road map for organizations to improve employee engagement, organizational effectiveness, and customer experience from vision through execution. To achieve these three goals simultaneously can be challenging, but Henkin and Bertels highlight that, with sustained effort and a long-term commitment, it is possible to have a more engaged workforce, a more effective organization, and a better customer experience. This is a must-have for your leadership library and an especially insightful tool for chief people officers!"

—**JULIE CATALANO,** chief people officer at Bespoke Partners

"Henkin and Bertels offer a masterful conversational dialogue about designing work that matters with a human-first mindset. *Fixing Work* offers timely perspective to organizations on the critical topic of designing work to attract, motivate, and retain a digital native workforce."

—BRIAN NEJMEH, senior operating partner at PeakEquity Partners and president of Instep

"I really enjoyed *Fixing Work*. As someone who has implemented transformations involving the design of new jobs across multiple areas, I found that the book portrayed a realistic journey and set of challenges to success. The ability to enhance service quality by empowering frontline workers to completely handle customer requests and align the organization to properly support that service delivery model will always elevate performance. It also creates competitive advantage in your market and a much more engaged workforce. I wish I had read *Fixing Work* before I took my journey, as it would have provided valuable insights about what to expect in driving this type of structural change."

—JOE SPADAFORD, president at J. Francis Consulting

"In *Fixing Work*, Henkin and Bertels dare to demystify the dark art of becoming strategic in your role. Read this if you intend to break out of the darkness."

—ED WALLACE, speaker, managing director of human capital at AchieveNEXT, and best-selling author of *The Relationship Engine*

"Is an engaging tale a great alternative to a corpspeak-laden business book on the meaning of work? Is the meaning revolution at work an unexpected pretext to write an engaging tale? Yes and yes! Dave and Thomas are the Shakespeare of management and the workplace. Leveraging a parable format, *Fixing Work* takes us on an actionable meditation with compelling situations where complicatedness is the wrong answer to complexity. They remind us about a powerful truth—that turning the corporate nonsense into a motivating, purposeful, discerning adventure for everyone is the noble quest of modern leaders."

—LAURENT CHOAIN, chief leadership of education and culture at Mazars

A Tale about Designing
Jobs Employees **Love**

FIXING
WORK

DAVID G. HENKIN &
THOMAS BERTELS

GREENLEAF
BOOK GROUP PRESS

Published by Greenleaf Book Group Press
Austin, Texas
www.gbgpress.com

Distributed by Greenleaf Book Group

For ordering information or special discounts for bulk purchases, please contact Greenleaf Book Group at PO Box 91869, Austin, TX 78709, 512.891.6100.

Design and composition by Greenleaf Book Group
Cover design by Greenleaf Book Group

Publisher's Cataloging-in-Publication data is available.

Print ISBN: 979-8-88645-077-4

eBook ISBN: 979-8-88645-078-1

To offset the number of trees consumed in the printing of our books, Greenleaf donates a portion of the proceeds from each printing to the Arbor Day Foundation. Greenleaf Book Group has replaced over 50,000 trees since 2007.

Printed in the United States of America on acid-free paper

23 24 25 26 27 28 29 30   10 9 8 7 6 5 4 3 2 1

First Edition

*To everyone striving to
improve the experience of work*

*To Kerra and Bradley
—David*

*To Theodore and Meisha
—Thomas*

CONTENTS

INTRODUCTION

High turnover. Low levels of employee engagement. Low productivity. Unclear accountabilities. Frustrated customers. These are all symptoms that tell us that in many organizations, work is fundamentally broken.

What is at the heart of this? A failure to design work for humans. Decades of research have shown again and again that we all want meaningful work, autonomy, and feedback, but only a small fraction of companies have incorporated these insights into the actual design of work to create intrinsically motivating, self-fulfilling jobs. The vast majority of companies today are stuck in an industrial, assembly-line-era mindset, in which a narrow focus on cost results in highly fragmented workflows and steep, often excessively multilayered hierarchies.

The opportunity to fix and redesign how we work is enormous, and companies that seize it will win the future. Those that don't will find it increasingly challenging to attract, engage, and retain top talent—and they will fall behind in both competitiveness and relevance in the modern age.

There is a better way. We wrote this book to provide people managers at all levels with a realistic example and practical road map for how to simultaneously improve employee engagement and motivation, organizational effectiveness and productivity, and customer experience and satisfaction. This story takes place in one company and one industry, but its concepts are applicable to every company in any industry. While the characters and events that appear here are imaginary, the workplace and environmental reality that produces them is authentic.

We hope you enjoy the journey, gain and apply useful ideas, and reap the many benefits of fixing work!

RISE AND SHINE

In the early Monday morning quiet, Jerry Crawford takes a deep breath. Awake before his alarm again, his eyes follow shadows across the room, and his mind is already thinking about the workweek ahead. As always, the weekend went by in a flash, and now it was back to the grind. Mindful not to wake his wife, Haley, Jerry silently slithers out of bed and makes his way to the kitchen.

Coffee in hand, he quickly scans through the emails on his phone. Fifty-nine new messages since he shut down the phone last night. Unbelievable. Fortunately, most of it is junk, but two messages catch his attention. The first one is a notice from the Human Resources department reminding him that performance reviews for his team are overdue. Jerry feels his blood pressure going up. As if he did not already have enough on his plate. He scrolls to the second message. Julia, arguably the best performer on his team, has sent an invitation for a meeting in what was the last open slot he had on his calendar all day. For a second, he contemplates declining the meeting invitation, but he knows that his schedule for the rest of the week is already packed as well. No point kicking the can down the road. He looks at this watch: time to get going. Atlanta traffic is no joke, and the sooner he gets to work, the better.

He puts his cup in the sink and heads for the shower. As he comes out, Haley is starting to wake up. She sends him off with a kiss and the same loving and inspiring message as always: "Be the author of your life. Go write your story forward."

Fifteen minutes later, he is on the road. On a good day, the commute from his home in Atlanta's Buckhead section to Consolidated Insurance's office south of the airport takes only twenty-five minutes, but today is not a good day. By the time he pulls into the parking lot, he is already running late for the weekly status conference call with the sales leadership team.

For Jerry, as the head of client onboarding, the meeting is only informational, and most of the discussion is usually irrelevant to him and his team. Still, he dislikes being late. He goes straight to his office, closes the door, and gets on the call.

Bellamy, the sales VP, is in the midst of a self-congratulatory speech about how successful the launch of the new life insurance product had been. *What a joke*, Jerry thinks—the product launch had been a complete fiasco. Jerry settles into his ergonomic chair and makes sure he is muted.

Consolidated Insurance is a midsize insurance company that sells employee benefits programs, with a focus on midsize companies. These companies could have anywhere from fifty to five hundred employees, and Cons (the company's humorous, if awkward, nickname) provides them with dental, disability, vision, and now also life insurance benefits.

The programs are sold through brokers, who are supported by regional sales offices. Once a client signs, Jerry's department is responsible for setting them up on the various internal data systems for billing and claims management—a complicated, arduous process made worse by computer systems that do not talk to each other and a sales department that routinely promises turnaround times that are completely unrealistic.

When he hears Bellamy mention his name, Jerry jumps up in his chair. "Jerry, could you give us an update on the status of client enrollment? Our account managers keep getting calls from clients and brokers about service issues. Maybe you can shed some light on that for us?"

Ouch. He quickly unmutes himself and responds as diplomatically as he can: "We are looking into what is going on, but we are short-staffed, and we need IT to fix the interface. And—"

Bellamy cuts him off: "Jerry, quite frankly, I don't care which dog ate your homework. I request that for our call next week, you give us an update on where we stand and how we will address these issues. Is that something you can do for us?"

Jerry immediately thinks of a few sharp-edged remarks he would like to say but knows better than to get into a pissing contest with Bellamy. "Of course, Bellamy, no problem."

He pushes the mute button again, as the meeting moves to another topic, and walks over to the huge whiteboard that takes up an entire wall of his office and which he uses to keep his top priorities visible. He adds "Service issue update for Monday sales meeting" and "Team performance reviews" to the list. Filling the team's two open positions is the most important issue, but the performance reviews and the service issue update he just promised Bellamy will require immediate action. Jerry sighs.

As he turns back to his desk, he sees Julia walking toward his office. He smiles. "Julia, how are you? How was your weekend?" Julia has been probably the best hire he ever made.

Smart, ambitious, focused, and energetic—she would certainly go places. Half a year ago, he had promoted her to the role of supervisor, which had turned out to be an excellent decision.

"It was nice, thank you. Gave me a little extra time to be sure about this conversation," Julia replies. She smiles fleetingly. "I'm sorry, Jerry, but another opportunity has come up, and I'm going to take it." She places a piece of paper onto his desk. It's her resignation letter.

Jerry feels flushed and unprepared—and a bit shocked, as he and Julia have had a great rapport. Or so he thought. "Wow, wow," Jerry blurts out. "Wow, okay. Julia, you're such an important member of the team. Is this something we can discuss?"

"Thanks, but no, I've made up my mind," Julia quickly replies. "I had higher hopes as well, and I really appreciated the promotion you gave me, but the last few months have been difficult. My notice period is two weeks, but I have a bunch of vacation days left that I would like to take. So, if it's all right with you, Jerry, I'd like to wrap things up by Thursday."

Jerry could only nod.

"I really appreciate all you did for me. I do wish you the best," Julia says, and just like that, she gets up and leaves his office.

Jerry looks at his whiteboard. Three openings now. He feels his pulse quicken.

While his department is frequently criticized for excessive delays in onboarding new clients, the quality issues certainly have gotten worse and are now also showing up in the monthly customer satisfaction survey. Most of the issues are simple mistakes like misspelled names on ID cards, but some of them are starting to have a negative impact on the Underwriting and Claims department. And, of course, Sales. Onboarding clients

- FILL 2 3 OPEN POSITIONS
- TEAM PERFORMANCE REVIEWS
- SERVICE ISSUE UPDATE FOR MONDAY SALES MEETING

is critical to facilitate billing them for the coverage. When his team falls behind, as it has recently, billing is delayed, which drives the sales folks crazy because they are counting on those fat commission checks. All of this also explains Bellamy's present antagonism toward Jerry, as well as that coming from several other upper-level management types in the company.

With three open positions, he knows he is in big trouble. There is simply no way his short-staffed department can tackle the workload in front of them. Everybody is already stretched to the max. He looks through the big glass wall of his office over three clusters of cubicles, one for each team.

The cubicles of three supervisors—Johnny, Mary, and Julia—are significantly larger than those of their team members. Johnny and Mary are both in their early forties. Between the two of them, Johnny is clearly the better coach. Mary drives her team hard, arguably too hard, but she drives herself hard as well. Both teams have open positions.

Johnny's team includes Dakota, Tatum, and Olivia. They

complement each other well. Dakota started only a few months ago, after graduating college. She had been an intern the summer before her senior year, and she seems to have hit the ground running. It has been two years since Tatum came on board. He is diligent, devotes high attention to detail, and is great with clients. Olivia is the longest tenured member of the team. She recently celebrated her twenty-year anniversary. Jerry likes Olivia a lot. She is like the organizational memory of the department—the historian, if you will—whom Jerry can always rely on to explain why things are being done a certain way. This also unfortunately means she is often quite resistant to change. He vividly remembers her response when soon after he joined Cons, he proposed they change the way they track the case status. While she had been very polite, she basically refused to even consider a different way of working. Sometimes, Olivia exhibits the classic "but we've always done it this way" mentality.

Mary's team is a somewhat different story. Skylar is a solid performer. She is in her mid-thirties and a proud mom of twin boys. Rasheed arrived the same month as Jerry. Rasheed is a smart fellow, though his true passion is to become a jazz musician rather than process spreadsheets all day (and who could blame him). Mary's team also includes Michele, who is early career, ambitious, analytical, and highly capable with high potential. She often shares her thoughts on how things might be improved, which Jerry really appreciates.

And finally, there is Julia's team: Ryan, Lee, Eric, and Hannah. Ryan and Lee are in their early thirties. Both are young parents, and both love sports. Ryan is a college football fanatic, whereas Lee loves baseball. Initially, Jerry was not impressed with either of them. But since Julia took over the team, he has noticed that both have seemed a lot more engaged. Eric is an interesting character. Jerry knows very little about him, and Eric seems intent on keeping it that way. Every attempt Jerry has made to learn more about him has been rebuffed. But Eric gets his work done. Hannah is the weakest member of the team, at least in Jerry's eyes. In her late thirties, she is constantly complaining about being underpaid and overworked. When Jerry announced Julia's promotion to supervisor, Hannah was visibly disappointed; it was abundantly clear that she had expected to be put in charge of the team. But Julia had managed to engage her somewhat successfully. And now Julia is gone. Jerry will probably have to step in and take over the group, at least until he finds a replacement.

Jerry's phone alerts him that it is time to get on his next call. The rest of the day passes quickly, with little time to work on the pressing issues staring at him from the whiteboard on the wall across from his desk. He even skips lunch in his effort to catch up on the most burning issues. Thankfully, by the time Jerry is able to leave the office, rush hour is over, though it's small reward for the kind of day he's had. He gets home in less than thirty minutes. As he walks through the door, Haley is preparing dinner.

"Perfect timing, honey! How was your day?"

"Well, Julia announced she is leaving," Jerry begins to share, "so now I have three open positions. The next couple of weeks will be tough."

Haley walks over and gives him a big hug. "You will figure something out, Jerry. You always do."

He nods, although the wry smile on his face surely gives him away. They sit down to eat dinner—a delicious red snapper with rice and sautéed carrots. But Jerry cannot stop thinking about work. How on earth is he going to sort this all out?

BUSINESS AS UNUSUAL

Tuesday is Jerry's least favorite day—jam-packed with meetings. By the time he heads over to the office of his boss, Cameron, for his weekly one-on-one, Jerry is exhausted. Cameron is Consolidated's vice president of Client Services, and one time when Haley asked Jerry to describe his boss in one word, the first word that came to his mind was "oblivious." A phrase would be "sunny-side up." Despite being mostly disengaged, Cameron always seems to come out on top. Jerry arrives at Cameron's office a little early, hoping to get some help with recruiting.

Cameron's office has nicer, if oddly uncomfortable, chairs and an outside window. He motions to Jerry to wait while he finishes a call. Jerry paces a bit, glancing back every few moments. Finally, Cameron waves him in. "Jerry, how are you? Nice to see you."

"Well, I've been better. I'm actually hoping to get some help. You probably heard that Julia has resigned. I'm very concerned about how that will affect our ability to keep up."

"I did hear, yes. She was sharp; we'll miss her. But it's so competitive now," Cameron offers.

Jerry continues, "We were already struggling to keep up as it is, and we're now dealing with three open requisitions. Is there any way we can get help? Our capacity is just not there, and the team overall is feeling it. I'm very concerned."

"Jerry, do you know what a rock tumbler is?" Cameron asks, taking the conversation in a different direction.

"Yes, I think so," Jerry replies.

"I just read this article. It mentions Steve Jobs. And it talked about a widowed man who lived up the street from Steve. One day he shows Steve an old, dusty rock tumbler. It was basically a motor and a coffee can and a little drive belt between them. Then they go out back and collect some rocks. Regular, plain, ugly old rocks."

"Okay," says Jerry.

"Well," Cameron continues, "next they put those plain rocks in the can with a little bit of liquid and a little bit of grit powder. Then they close the can, and the older man turns this motor on. The contraption starts making a lot of noise, and the older man tells Jobs to come back tomorrow."

"Okay," monotones Jerry, as Cameron pauses.

"So, Steve comes back the next day. They open the can and take out amazingly polished, beautiful rocks. The same plain stones, bumping, friction, time, and voilà!"

"Okay," says Jerry a third time, now getting quietly irritated. "I get the concept, but I'm not sure how that applies here, now? We need to fill our reqs and—"

"Jerry, I've got another meeting starting shortly here," Cameron interjects. "Take that friction and make something beautiful out of it!" Cameron turns away from Jerry toward his computer, abruptly signaling that their meeting is over.

As Jerry walks back to his office, his dread only grows. Not entirely surprised by how unhelpful Mr. Sunny-Side Up was, he is nonetheless disappointed.

"Hey, Jerry, how's life?" chirps Elrod Tubbs. Elrod works in Cons' IT department, responsible for the data group. He and Elrod talk with some regularity as Jerry's team has frequent data issues and much of their process involves data and systems. In Jerry's early days Elrod had helped explain much of the systems and dataflows. However, as Jerry dug in and asked about improvements and upgrades, especially as the business grew and Jerry's team grew, Elrod had become less helpful. Things had come to a boil the last time they met, when in response to a question from Jerry about the status of the life product implementation, Elrod had asked him to submit a ticket via the IT service desk. Jerry had come close to losing his temper.

Feigning inner calm, Jerry responds, "Not too bad, Elrod. How about yourself?"

Elrod smiled. "Doing great. With the life product implementation done, we can finally get back to working on the new claims system. That will be a monster, but we hope to get the funding approved next month."

"A new claims system? But what about the data integration work we requested?"

"Well, Jerry, that work has been put on hold," Elrod replies. "Gordon has asked us to prioritize the new system above everything else, so we put all other requests on hold. Plus, there is no funding for that."

Jerry could not believe what he had just heard. "Seriously? We are drowning in work as it is, and the interface breakdowns are one of the biggest problems we are facing. Isn't there anything you can do?"

Was that a smirk on Elrod's face? "Sorry, Jerry, take a number. But the claims project is the future of the company—and I am quoting Gordon here. You—meaning you specifically—will have to make do. Anyway, nice seeing you!"

In point of fact, Elrod actually works for Ben, Cons' chief information officer or CIO. So he is not exactly at the top of the corporate food chain, and in fact, he and Jerry are essentially peers. *Dropping Gordon's name so flippantly seems a bit much*, Jerry thinks. Gordon is Cons' CEO, and it is not likely that Elrod will be joining Gordon for drinks and golf at the country club anytime soon.

By now Jerry's mood had turned sour. With Cons' profitability declining over recent years, Gordon had invested heavily into updating its ancient systems, but instead of improving things, it had only increased the workload. Many of the new systems did not connect with what was already in place. Jerry had spent many hours with Elrod trying to understand and improve the situation, without much success to show for it.

Jerry briefly contemplates talking to Bellamy. As the head of Sales, Bellamy has a vested interest in the performance of Jerry's group. But given how the call at the start of the week went, that seems risky. Jerry looks at his whiteboard. He still needs to put together an explanation of the service issues for Bellamy by Monday. There was no point in starting to work on that tonight; it was already way too late. He heads home, zombielike in the evening darkness.

As Jerry approaches their house, he realizes he forgot to give Haley a heads-up that he would be running late. As he enters, Haley is just cleaning up the kitchen.

"Sorry, honey, but work is a bit crazy these days," Jerry confesses. "I am down three people, and I completely forgot."

Haley shrugs and points to the oven. "I made lasagna," she says flatly. "Your portion is in the oven." Haley works from home as a computer programmer. Their time together has always been a priority for both of them, even if it might simply consist of having dinner together in the evening.

Jerry feels her disappointment. Haley heads to bed while Jerry is still eating. By the time he joins her, Haley is already sound asleep. But sleep doesn't come easily for Jerry. Thoughts race through his mind, but they keep looping back to the stupid rock tumbler story Cameron had told him. By the time Jerry falls asleep, it's way past midnight.

The next day, Wednesday, is highlighted by Jerry's monthly staff meeting. The meeting is deliberately scheduled to be brief: only half an hour. On his drive to work, he thinks about how to make use of the limited time, deciding that he will go straight to business and try to hit the problems head-on. As he walks into the large conference room, his entire team is already waiting for him.

"Good morning, everybody. I know we have a huge caseload to work through, so I want to keep this short and sweet. But I have three things I want to talk about. One is recognizing Julia, who is leaving us. Julia, we will miss you." He pauses for a moment.

Judging from the looks on their faces, they all already knew.

"Ryan, Lee, Eric, and Hannah," Jerry continues, "I will be filling in for Julia until we can find a replacement. For now, please put a weekly meeting for the five of us on my calendar."

He looks over to Julia's team and sees heads nodding.

"Second, we need to get these performance reviews done. Johnny and Mary, please make sure you get yours done before the end of next week. Ryan, Lee, Eric, and Hannah, I will be doing yours." Jerry sees heads nodding in grim affirmation again.

"And third, as you know, we are a bit behind." Jerry scans the room. "With Julia leaving, we now have three open positions and a backlog of 270 cases. I need to give Sales an update on where we stand and how we plan to address that issue. And that is what I would like to talk about for the rest of this meeting."

Nobody says anything for a few seconds. Mary breaks the silence. "Well, that is actually not true."

Jerry looks at her cautiously.

"Our case backlog as of today is 297. I just got a ton of new contracts from National Accounts. They have been busy!" Mary says.

Ouch, Jerry thinks. He clears his throat. "Well, so what are we going to do about that? Any bright ideas?"

Ryan is the next to say something. "Well, this might be a little bit contentious. But if we all could focus on the simple cases and hold off the complex ones for a few weeks, we could probably reduce the backlog and at least make our numbers look better."

Not a bad idea, Jerry muses, but obviously risky. Frustrating the large customers even more would be a surefire way to antagonize Sales. Obviously, Ryan was trying to be pragmatic, if not also provocative, and hey, at least somebody chimed in with an idea. In an effort to be supportive and spur more ideas, Jerry walks over to his flipchart. He grabs a marker and jots Ryan's idea down:

- *Process simple cases first*

He turns around, looking at the group. "Any other ideas? Nothing is off limits."

Johnny raises his hand. "What about training? If everybody was familiar with every system, the whole scheduling work would be much easier."

A bit self-serving, Jerry thinks, since scheduling is one of Johnny's main responsibilities. And it's also not very realistic, given the patchwork of systems and the time it takes to train people on them. But Jerry adds the idea to the flipchart anyway:

- *Cross-training on systems*

To Jerry's surprise, Olivia raises her hand. "Yes, Olivia?"

Olivia carefully shares, "How about we stop asking employers to validate the census before we load the data into the system?"

Oh boy. Jerry knows all too well that, given the long time span between when employers submit their census data to get a quote and when Cons enters the information into its systems, the census information is usually out of date. Some employees at those companies will have left, and new hires will very likely have been added. Simply taking the initial census would, of course, save a lot of time but also create a lot of problems later on for Customer Service. Talk about kicking the can down the road. But regardless of what he thinks about this particular idea, Jerry adds it to the list. After all, he had offered that nothing is off limits:

- *Stop validating census*

Jerry looks at the clock. Only two minutes left. "Well, we won't solve this today, but I would appreciate if you all think about it some more. Please add any additional ideas to the flip-chart, and we will talk more about this over the next few weeks." Team members gather their things and start shuffling their way out of their chairs. "Back to work, folks. Thank you." Jerry closes the meeting.

The room empties out quickly, except for Johnny and Mary. "Jerry, do you have a few minutes?" Johnny asks.

Jerry's next meeting was not for another half hour, so he nods yes.

"Great," Johnny replies and then clears his throat. "Well, I did not want to bring this up in the meeting, but you will hear this anyway. We have a major problem with the life product. It turns out that the interface between the life platform and the policy admin system is not working properly. So, as it stands, the data does not come over. It looks like IT dropped the ball again."

Jerry cannot believe what he's just heard. "Did nobody test the workflow before we went live?"

Mary jumps in. "Jerry, we did not. As you might recall, there was this huge push to hit the go-live date. Everybody was scrambling up to the last minute. And Elrod signed off on it!"

Wow. Really. Jerry thinks for a second about calling Elrod to find out why he'd signed off. Did he even check or validate anything?

But given his last exchange with Elrod, it would mostly not be a good use of time. *How much worse can this week get?* Jerry thinks. If what Mary and Johnny said was true, then they would have to check all the cases they had already completed.

"How many—" Jerry starts.

Mary does not wait until he finishes the question. "About eighty cases, Jerry."

"So why did we not find out about this sooner?" Jerry asks, mindful of his tone and trying mightily not to admonish the messengers.

"Well, remember our backlog?" Mary replies. "We launched the life product back in October. And the first deals came in sometime later that month. But since our backlog is so humongous, we just now completed the enrollment of the first groups. And when we did the final check of the policy documents and created the first bill, we realized that life was missing."

Jerry sighs. "Well, at least we did not send anything out to a client, right?"

"Correct," Mary states. "But we need to rework all eighty cases. And since the interface is not working, that will require a lot of manual data entry."

"How long do you think it will take to work through this?" Johnny chimes in.

"Well, it would probably take three people two weeks to get it all sorted out," Mary answers firmly.

Jerry's chin drops. "Johnny, that means your entire team does nothing else for two weeks."

Johnny nods. "That's right, boss."

"Okay, I need to process that," Jerry says, placing both hands on his temples. Johnny and Mary nod and leave the room.

Back in his office, Jerry walks over to his whiteboard and adds "Fix 80 life cases."

Jerry grimaces. This is becoming overwhelming. They were behind as it was. The life problem just sets them back even further. And the only ideas that would relieve the pressure in the short run would create even bigger problems in the long run.

- FILL 2 3 OPEN POSITIONS
- TEAM PERFORMANCE REVIEWS
- SERVICE ISSUE UPDATE FOR MONDAY SALES MEETING
- FIX 80 LIFE CASES

And even if he could fill the three open positions right away, it would take weeks if not months before the new team members would be able to relieve some of the pressures. There was no way out. He would have to talk to Bellamy. Well, first he would have to talk to Cameron to let him know what was going on. Could this week, indeed, get any worse?

By the time Jerry leaves the office, the parking lot is once again empty under the glare of the halogen street lamps. At least today he remembered to call Haley early enough to let her know that he would be late. By the time he gets home, she is already in her pajamas, reading a book in front of the fireplace.

She gets up and gives him a hug. "Sounds like you had another rough day. Well, we have some leftover lasagna from yesterday. It's warming in the oven. Go and eat! And join me afterward."

After he finishes eating, he rinses off the dishes, leaving them in the sink, and joins Haley in front of the fire.

She looks up from her book. "Ready to go to bed?"

"Yes, ma'am, I am done. This was another day from hell."

Haley smiles. "You will figure it out, honey. I have no doubts."

"Well, from your lips to God's ears."

They go upstairs, brush their teeth, and climb into bed. Haley gives him a kiss, and seconds later Jerry is fast asleep.

EMPTY CANS RATTLE

Throughout his academic career, Jerry was a decent student for the most part. He mostly steered clear of trouble, too. His middle school science teacher, Mr. Paco, once told him, "Empty cans rattle the loudest. Don't bother blathering all about; say things of value!" That message stuck with Jerry: He tries to be intentional and purposeful when he talks. On Friday of a long, hard week, he is reminded of Mr. Paco's words when Bob, his department's human resources business partner (HRBP), loops back to him the day after his exit interview with Julia.

"So, another one out the door," Bob starts. "TGIF, Jerry. I've been doing a few of these lately, and it's the same as everybody else: new opportunity, better prospects, blah, blah, blah."

Jerry is indignant with Bob's cavalier attitude. "Julia was a high performer, with high potential," he interjects. "Tell me, Bob, did you learn anything that can help us better retain the talent we have? And perhaps better recruit as well? I now have three open roles I need to fill. Urgently, too."

Bob just shrugs, "Everybody has the same challenges, Jerry. It's hard to find good people these days!"

"Can we get the talent acquisition team to up their game? Why aren't we more competitive? Are we paying enough?" Jerry asks, knowing it's likely rhetorical, given his experience with Bob.

"Look, Jerry," Bob retorts, "we actually pay quite a bit above market. We have the same problem in nearly every department. Turnover is at an all-time high. I shouldn't tell you yet, but the results of the annual engagement survey are back—and they are bad. I am sure we will see some changes coming through. They are talking about more flextime, remote work at least for some roles, and casual dress. Maybe that will address the issue. The executive team is taking the first stab at this, and Cameron should be sharing more information soon. But as I said, the numbers don't look good."

Every few years, Cons' HR department conducts an employee engagement survey to measure the "health" of the connection the company's employees have toward their work, their immediate team, and the organization as a whole, as well as to try to examine the factors that influence those feelings and attitudes. And every few years, Jerry and his peers hear the dismal results.

Bob and Jerry adjourn, with Jerry more concerned than ever. Their backlog of cases had been growing steadily and was likely to get worse with Julia leaving. A year ago, they had 150 open cases, and now that number had grown to 270—well actually, almost 300, according to Mary. Jerry knew that they could complete, on average, twenty-five cases a week, and if his math was right, that would increase the time from deal closed to client setup complete to about three months. Clients would be furious. Customer Service would be drowning in calls. And with no data in the system, the Claims team would have to manually review every single claim. It was imperative that he get more resources, but HR could not even fill the open positions he had. And even if he could find the right talent tomorrow, it would take months before they were up to speed.

Sitting alone in his office after the meeting with Bob, Jerry decides to come clean. He knows that Bellamy does not like surprises. Waiting until Monday to drop the bomb that not only will things not improve but they will probably get worse is not an option.

Jerry runs into Cameron on his way back from lunch and tries to explain the life fiasco. But Cameron is distracted. When Jerry mentions that Bellamy is expecting a report as to what they would do to fix the client experience, Cameron simply nods and says, "I trust you, Jerry. You'll do the right thing." Jerry hears this as code for "You are on your own, buddy!" *Oh well, Cameron being Cameron*, Jerry cynically concludes.

He is dreading picking up the phone to call Bellamy to break the news, when Johnny and Tatum knock at his door. "Got a second for us?"

Jerry sighs. "Sure, guys, come on in. What can I do for you?"

Johnny is grinning ear to ear, which seems strange, given the trouble they are in. *Has he snapped?* Jerry wonders.

"Tatum has something he wants to show you," says Johnny.

Tatum seems nervous but excited. "Jerry, how much do you know about robots?"

Jerry looks incredulous. "What do you mean?"

"Well, I am a bit of a tech geek," Tatum continues, "and

I have been looking into RPA to see if that is something we can use."

The confused look on Jerry's face is not lost on Tatum, so he quickly carries on. "RPA, meaning robotic process automation, is an approach to automate repetitive tasks. Tasks such as data entry. Since our meeting on Wednesday, Johnny and I have been exploring whether we can use it to automate the data entry for the missing life policies. And we think we figured out a way to do it. You wanna see?"

Jerry jumps up. "Of course I do. Show me!"

They walk over to Tatum's desk. As they get closer, Jerry sees that something strange is going on. On Tatum's screen, he sees a screen opening up and data being entered, and then another screen opening up and more data being entered. It looks like the computer is possessed.

"Looks like a virus!" Jerry utters, confused.

"Well, what you see is the bot working. I created a short program that basically copies the data from the life platform to the policy admin system," Tatum explains. Johnny nods his head.

Jerry is stunned. "So, wait, what does that mean?"

Tatum grins. "Well, as I said, the computer is doing all the work. At this stage, we are halfway through the backlog."

Jerry can't believe what he's just heard. "So we won't need three people for two weeks?"

"Correct. If I am not mistaken, we will be done by tomorrow afternoon. The computer will keep on working through the weekend," Tatum smiles as he explains.

Jerry feels a strong urge to hug Tatum but catches himself just in time. "This is fantastic. Tatum, well done. Really well done!"

Johnny chimes in, "I asked Elrod about RPA months ago. He never made time for it. Tatum jumped right in, and—bam!—" Johnny claps his hands, "just like that, we are up and running! And Tatum has some other ideas for how we can use RPA to help us with some of the other manual processes."

Finally, a light at the end of the tunnel! "Guys, this is the best news I have had all week. Tatum, please make this a priority. Johnny, can you ensure that Tatum has time to work on this?"

Back in his office, Jerry ponders his next move. Obviously, this does not solve the backlog problem, at least not right away, but it represents a step in the right direction. Though when Elrod finds out, that will probably turn into yet another problem. When it came to technology, he was quite territorial—when it suited his agenda.

Jerry picks up the phone and punches in Bellamy's extension. He hears Bellamy's voicemail. Jerry decides to leave a message, although he would have preferred to talk with him in person.

"Hey, Bellamy, this is Jerry. I'm calling about the update on the service issues you requested for Monday, and . . . and I need a bit more time. I totally understand your concerns, and of course we want to make the clients happy. But there is no silver bullet. That said, we have some ideas for how we could approach the situation. And I was wondering if I could get some time with you next week to discuss what makes the most sense. When you have a second, please call me back. You can reach me on my cell phone anytime." Jerry leaves his number and hangs up. Then he looks up at the clock, shocked to see it's already 5:00 p.m.—it's been that kind of week.

There's no point staying in the office and nothing further he can do at this point, so Jerry decides to leave the office early—well, at least earlier than most days this week.

Of course, Jerry gets stuck in Friday rush hour traffic. It takes him nearly ninety minutes to get home. But today he does not mind. It gives him time to think. Tatum had really saved him and his team today. Who knew he was such a computer genius? Maybe the team could leverage Tatum's skills with some of the other challenges as well.

When he gets home, the house is empty, a note on the fridge from Haley. "Meeting my friend Anna tonight for drinks and dinner," it read. "You are on your own. Love, Haley."

Next to the note was a menu for the local pizza delivery place. Jerry decides to order a calzone and open a bottle of wine—well deserved after a rough and roller-coaster week.

UNEXPECTED ENCOUNTER

Feeling bad about how little time he spent with Haley during the week, Jerry wants to make up for it this weekend. And he has a plan: Haley loves fresh croissants, and Jerry discovered a while back that Atlanta's best croissants are made fresh daily at a tiny Korean bakery in Duluth. So, bright and early on Saturday morning he heads to Duluth. At 7:30 a.m., it's sunny but quite cold, and Jerry is thankful that the line at the bakery is mercifully short.

As he pays for four croissants, Jerry hears someone call his name.

"Jerry Crawford?"

Jerry turns around. At first, he doesn't recognize the thin man standing behind him. But then the penny drops. Mike Cuthbert!

Cuthbert was at Georgia Tech around the same time Jerry finished his degree. They had taken some of the same classes together. But Cuthbert had dropped out of the program to start a business. He soon made headlines when his first venture, a platform for marathon runners, was acquired by a leading footwear brand for $20 million. Jerry still remembers the envy he felt when reading the profile in the alumni magazine a few years back. If Jerry remembered correctly, Cuthbert had started and sold several other ventures since. A bona fide serial entrepreneur.

"Mike, so nice to see you! It has been a while. How are you?" Jerry says, opening his hand to embrace Cuthbert's outstretched hand.

Cuthbert smiles. "Not too bad. Wanna grab a coffee and catch up?"

They order two lattes and sit down at one of the small bistro tables.

"So, what are you up to these days?" Jerry asks.

"Jerry, I can tell you—but then I would have to kill you!" Cuthbert grins. "But seriously, I can't tell you specifics. My new venture is still in stealth mode. But what I can tell you is that we are trying to fix work using data."

Jerry is intrigued. "What do you mean by 'fixing work'?"

Cuthbert takes a big sip of his latte. "Well, you might recall that I started a few companies and that I was lucky enough to sell most of them."

Jerry nods.

"Well, you probably know this," Cuthbert continues, "but when you sell a business like that, the deal contains an earn-out clause. You basically get your money over time, provided the business continues to perform."

"The famous golden handcuffs. Of course."

"Exactly. So," Cuthbert lowers his voice a little, "I started three businesses, and every one of them I sold to a large company. And in each case, I was stuck working in these larger organizations for a few years until I got my money out. And I realized during each of those earn-out periods how painful it is to work in those organizations, or I should say, to work *for* those organizations."

"Oh, I can relate," Jerry commiserates.

Cuthbert continues, "I mean, these were very well-run businesses. But for an entrepreneur, being stuck inside a structure like that is almost like being paralyzed. I felt like a small cog in a giant machine. The bureaucracy was overwhelming. I knew I was the lucky one, the one who would walk out the door after two years with a ton of cash. But I started to really feel for the people inside those organizations, how they were just kinda stuck there, working in outdated structures and processes that often destroy any motivation. So, long story short, my new venture focuses on measuring how well designed the work is and identifying how that job could be improved to deliver a better employee experience. And my goal is to try to provide guidance and solutions for leaders who want to do something about that."

"Wow," Jerry says, intrigued. "So what does that actually mean? Is this some kind of engagement survey? We just did one of those at my company."

Cuthbert laughs. "Not really. Engagement surveys are a good idea, don't get me wrong, but we are aiming at something quite different. You are managing people, right?"

"Yes, I am. I have a team of fifteen," Jerry answers. "Well actually, twelve right now, since I have three open positions."

Cuthbert leans forward. "So how did you design the work your people do?"

Puzzled, Jerry asks, "What do you mean by 'designing'? The job descriptions?"

Cuthbert laughs. "Sure, let's go with that. How did you design the jobs by way of those descriptions?"

"Well, to tell you the truth," Jerry replies, "I did not design them. They already existed when I took over the department."

Cuthbert sighs. "Well, you are not alone. Most managers I meet spend very little time thinking about the design of the actual jobs. It's rare to find a manager who is excited about creating a job description. Most of the time, we copy and paste what we used in another company. Maybe tweak it a little bit. And that is part of the problem."

"What do you mean?"

"Well, for one, these days we are in really fierce competition for talent. You mentioned you have three open positions, right?"

Jerry nods.

"Tell me. How easy is it to fill them?"

Jerry shakes his head. "Really hard—although we pay very well. Or so I'm told," he adds, thinking back to HRBP Bob's remark that Cons pays over market.

Cuthbert nods. "Well, good pay is fine, Jerry, but in this day and age, maybe you need to think about the jobs you offer as a product itself. How competitive is the product? How well designed is it to meet the needs of the consumer? The employee, in this case."

Confused, Jerry asks, "Work as a product? Employees as consumers? Slow down. What do you mean?"

Cuthbert laughs. "I understand your reaction. It is a rather unusual way to look at work. Hey, I would love to chat more, but I have a commitment at 9:00 a.m. and I better get going. But certainly, happy to connect another time." Cuthbert pushes his chair back and gathers his things. "Great to see you after all these years, Jerry!"

"Mike, same here. And I would definitely love to get your

perspective on the challenges I am facing at work. I think what you are talking about is certainly part of the problem."

Mike laughs again. "The solution," he says. "What I'm talking about is the solution. But sure, anytime, Jerry. Let's get together again. Here is my number. Just text me." Handing Jerry a business card, Cuthbert gets up, shakes Jerry's hand again, and is out the door.

Jerry grabs his croissants and heads home, with pieces of the conversation bouncing around in his head.

Before the day ends, he texts Cuthbert and they agree to meet again, this time over a beer in downtown Atlanta.

THE HARD WAY

Jerry is nearly at the office Monday morning before realizing he never heard back from Bellamy. He's a bit nervous dialing into the weekly sales call but is relieved when Brian, the head of National Accounts, opens the call by announcing that Bellamy is away, attending a conference in Texas.

The service topic does not come up during the call. Instead, the discussion focuses on the new commission scheme Sales is rolling out. Jerry checks his schedule for the rest of the day. He is eager for the evening to arrive and with it, his next meeting with Cuthbert.

When, after another very long day of meetings, Jerry arrives at the Irish pub, Cuthbert is already waiting for him.

"Mike, good to see you again," Jerry offers as they shake hands. "So good to run into you on Saturday. Our conversation gave me plenty to think about."

Cuthbert laughs. "Well, Jerry, let's get you a beer first." He waives the waiter over, and they order.

Jerry takes a breath and then launches into the problem at hand. "Okay. I'm dealing with a difficult situation at work. We have more work than we can handle, and the team is stressed.

To make matters worse, we just had a star performer leave, and there are so many areas to improve. And maybe on top of it all, I can't seem to get my management to engage or help much!"

"Sounds like a handful of trouble indeed," Cuthbert says.

"And what you said about designing work really resonated," Jerry says, trying to sound as genuine as he felt. "Maybe we can explore that a bit further?"

"With pleasure, Jerry," Cuthbert says, "but before we dive into work design, maybe you could tell me a bit more about the context. Why don't you walk me through the work you and your team are doing, at a high level?"

"Sure thing. As I might have mentioned in our chat on Saturday morning, I work for Consolidated Insurance, where I am responsible for client onboarding. The whole company has about a thousand employees. I am in the benefits division, and I have a team of fifteen, although right now it's actually twelve, because I have a few open positions. You probably know this, but employee benefits are a crucial tool for employers to attract and retain their workers."

"Of course." Cuthbert nods.

Jerry continues, "So the way the process works is essentially this: First, somebody in HR in some company reaches out to a broker asking for a quote. The broker collects some key information and forwards that information along to us, underwriting gets involved to price it out, and the regional sales office sends the quote to the broker. When the client selects us, the sales office collects some additional data—for example, a census of all employees to be covered in the plan—and sends the whole package to us."

"Okay, I'm tracking with you so far," Cuthbert says.

"Our job is then to take all that information and set up the employer and the employees on our systems. We do this so that we can send bills and process claims when they come in. At the end of the process, we create the first bill and provide the client with an overview of the coverage. Now, what makes our work so difficult is that, depending on the product, we have different systems. The information coming in is often incomplete or incorrect, and we are constantly waiting for either the client, or the broker, or the account manager to provide some missing data."

"So how long does it take for your team to do their part of the process?" Cuthbert asks.

"Oh, that can range from two weeks up to two or three months."

"I see," Cuthbert replies. "And how is your team organized? I think you mentioned your department has fifteen people. Are they all doing the same work?"

"Well," Jerry shares, "in theory we would have fifteen people, but as I mentioned, we are down three. They are organized into three teams, and each handles separate functions: Mary's team receives the documentation and does the first quality check. If anything is incorrect or missing, they are the ones that resolve the issue. When everything is complete, they then hand over the work to Johnny's team, which manually enters the information into the various systems. When that part is done, Julia's team creates the first bill and the implementation package for the client."

"So it takes at least one person from each team to do the entire process?" Cuthbert asks.

"Well, not really," Jerry explains, "because our systems are so complex and not everybody is trained on every system, it can take up to six people to process a complicated case. And, of course, the supervisors are also involved, reviewing and checking their team's work."

"That must be really difficult to manage."

"You got that right!" Jerry agrees. "The supervisors are critical to make sure the workload is balanced and assigned to the right individual, to prioritize which case to work on next, and to measure performance."

Cuthbert smiles. "Thank you for explaining. That is very helpful. You mentioned at the beginning of our conversation that you are facing some challenges? Tell me more about that."

"Well, we currently face a tremendous backlog of cases. We could probably handle it if we were fully staffed, but I have two open frontline positions, and last week one of my supervisors resigned—which, by the way, means that, in addition to everything else on my plate, I need to manage her team until we get a replacement."

Cuthbert nods. "From where I am sitting you have options, at least two: the easy way and the hard way."

Jerry laughs. "Okay, I pick the easy way."

Cuthbert looks at him with a big smirk on his face. "Okay, so here it is: You need to add more people. Probably more than the three open positions you have, given how far you seem to be falling behind. And you should reset management's expectations so that they know that things will be difficult for a very long time."

Jerry is stunned. "You call that the easy way? I doubt I'd get more head count. I'm struggling to fill the three open positions. And forget about lowering expectations. That won't fly with upper management."

Cuthbert nods sympathetically. "I understand. Believe me. So maybe we should explore the hard way?"

"So, what's the hard way?" Jerry's tense voice gives away his sense of frustration.

Cuthbert looks him straight in the eye. "Fix the work itself."

"What do you mean by that?"

"You can only do a good job if there is a good job to be done," Cuthbert posits. "Would you agree?"

Jerry nods but is a little confused. "Sure," he replies.

Cuthbert grins again. "So, Jerry, tell me: What makes a good job?"

Jerry thinks about it for a few seconds and then asks, more than declares: "A competitive salary, good benefits, a supportive boss?"

Cuthbert shakes his head. "Well, those factors are obviously important, but that is not what I mean. What about the work itself?"

"Hmm," Jerry reflects.

"Jerry, think about all the jobs you've ever had," Cuthbert says. "Can you identify the one you enjoyed the most?

Jerry runs through his resume in his mind. He worked as an ice cream vendor in high school and had an internship at a financial industry brokerage house during his college years. He did a tour as a middle school teacher after college before deciding to shift and join the corporate ranks. He worked at a regional insurance processing house for a few years before coming over to Cons four years ago.

"As I step back and think about it," Jerry offers, "interestingly, I'd say teaching was probably the best job I've ever had."

"And why is that?"

"Well, first of all, it was really rewarding to see those kids grow. The classroom was fairly low tech, but we had what we needed. And it was really up to me to figure out the best way to help them learn. And I learned a lot, too."

"So the work was meaningful, and you had autonomy. Did you know how you were doing?"

"Actually, yes. After a couple of months, it was pretty obvious what worked and what did not, and how to adjust my approach to help everybody learn."

"Congratulations, you just discovered the secret formula for creating motivating work."

Jerry is perplexed. "What do you mean?"

"Well, as I said earlier, you can only do a good job if there is a good job to be done," Cuthbert reiterates. "For a job to qualify as 'good,' meaning intrinsically motivating, it needs to meet three criteria. The first one is that you have autonomy—you are able to make decisions and use your own judgment for how and when to do the work. The second one is knowledge of results—a fancy term for feedback—which is critical to be able to learn and improve. And the third one is that you experience the work to be meaningful."

"Okay, but what exactly do you mean by meaningful?" Jerry asks.

"Excellent question. There are also three parts to this. The first is that you get to use a variety of different skills and competencies. Think about when you were teaching. What skills did that require?"

"Let's see," Jerry considers. "Well for one, I had to figure out a way to make the topic interesting, not an easy task if you are dealing with thirteen-year-olds. And then I had to make sure everybody was engaged. And, of course, every kid is different. So you need to figure out several different ways to make the same point, just so that everybody gets it. It was not easy. And you know, even though I was the teacher, I really learned a lot myself in the process."

"Yes, that sounds like you had a lot of variety," Cuthbert says. "The second element is task identity: doing a job from start to finish. Being responsible for the entire work product."

"Okay, that makes sense, too," Jerry says, "because I owned the history and geography part of their report cards."

"Exactly." Cuthbert nods emphatically, throwing his hands in the air. "And the last component of meaningful work is task significance—that the work you do matters."

"Well, I hope my work made a difference," Jerry shares. "I believe it did."

"Jerry, I am sure it did," Cuthbert insists. "It certainly seems it made a difference to you."

"Okay, I am following you so far. But what do meaningful work, autonomy, and feedback have to do with my challenges at Cons?"

Cuthbert laughs. "Well, there are a couple of layers to that. Let's unpack this a bit more. The way most companies typically organize work does not pay attention to the needs of employees for a good job, and by a good job, I mean a fulfilling one, a job that is intrinsically motivating. That's really the bottom line. The approach most businesses use today is based on how industry used to organize work in the factories: They break the work into smaller pieces that require only a narrow set of skills, which allows companies to pay employees less. But to manage these employees and coordinate the work, you need a layer of supervisors to tell everybody what to do, how to do it, and when to do it, and check whether it was done right. And when you organize work that way, not only does it lead to employees experiencing their work as less motivating, but it also deals a blow to productivity."

Jerry was stunned. "What do you mean?"

"Well, there are several reasons why productivity suffers. First of all, breaking work into smaller pieces creates handoffs, which need to be managed. Second, accountability gets diffused—nobody feels accountable for the work product from start to finish. Third, you now need supervisors to oversee and provide feedback to those doing the work. Supervisors are expensive! Fourth, the time it takes to do the work actually increases, given all the handoffs and stages of production. And finally, it creates separation from the external customer."

Jerry has a light-bulb moment. "So let me play this back to you, just to make sure I understand correctly. You are saying that making the jobs better improves productivity?"

Cuthbert nods emphatically. "Indeed. What you have just described to me is a very fragmented workflow. I think if you could change the design of the work so that one person or a team does the entire case from start to finish, I bet you would see a tremendous increase both in productivity and in employee satisfaction. But let me warn you—that is not an easy journey."

Jerry's mind is racing.

Cuthbert continues, "Let me ask you this. If you think about the jobs in your department, how well do you think they score if you apply the criteria of meaningful work, autonomy, and feedback?"

Jerry ponders for a moment before responding. "Well, let's see. I mean, each of the three teams owns their part of the process, but they probably do not feel responsible for the entire process start to finish. But the variety of skills required is pretty high, just given the number of products and systems we have. Oh, and in terms of significance, I am sure everyone on my team knows how important their work is."

"Well, if that is true, congrats," Cuthbert says. "But be careful. If I were working on your team, I might see things very differently. But anyway, what about the other two components: autonomy and feedback?"

"Hmm . . . autonomy is somewhat limited, I have to admit. I mean, we need processes and controls. But feedback is not a problem. I mean, we have an annual performance review process. Hey, we are currently in the middle of doing performance reviews right now."

"Jerry, if I was working in your department, how would I know whether I am doing a good job?" Cuthbert asks plainly.

"Well, that is the supervisor's responsibility," Jerry responds.

"Unfortunately," Cuthbert says firmly, "that is only the third-best way to get feedback."

Jerry looks surprised. "What do you mean? What are the alternatives?"

Cuthbert smiles. "Did you need a supervisor to tell you that you were doing a good job when you were a teacher? But let's explore that another time. Based on what you told me, you might have an opportunity here to improve not only productivity but also motivation."

After a brief pause, Jerry nods his head. "I think you are right. But how do I get started?"

Cuthbert chuckles. "A bias for action—I like that. Well, I suggest you start with really understanding how your team spends its time."

The puzzled look on Jerry's face speaks volumes, so Cuthbert continues. "Well, you have a capacity challenge—so maybe before reorganizing the work, you might want to question whether you need to do all the things you do. What I am proposing is that you put together a list of what your department does, how much time is spent doing each item, and whether you need to do each of those items in the first place."

Still confused, Jerry interjects, "But I told you what we are doing—we are onboarding clients. That is all we do."

Cuthbert grins ear to ear. "So, what you are telling me is that every single minute of your employees' workday is spent on processing client cases? No meetings, no reports, no team interactions, no nothing?"

Jerry realizes that Cuthbert is right. There are quite a few things his department does routinely that have nothing to do with client service. "Okay, you got a point. But how does creating an inventory of the work we do help with my issue?"

"Once you have that list, let's meet again. It should take no more than a week to put together a list of the activities and the time required. Oh, and keep in mind: 'Only the wearer knows where the shoe pinches.'"

"Wait. What?" Jerry asks.

"Only the wearer knows where the shoe pinches," Cuthbert repeats. "It is also known as the iceberg of ignorance. The team leaders at the top only know about 4 percent of what is going on, but those doing the work know 100 percent. They know where the challenges and opportunities exist. They also know—all too well, I'm afraid—where the logjams and pressure points and problem areas are. Managers don't wear their employees' shoes, so they don't know where the 'pinch' is, simply because they don't do the work! So, what I am suggesting to you—what is in fact imperative—is that you make sure to engage your team in this little exercise."

"Humph," Jerry utters as he processes the points. "I could start a task list for the process and ask team members to chime in?" he muses, thinking aloud.

"Good idea," Cuthbert affirms. "Maybe form a team that includes employees and supervisors? That will help make sure you don't miss anything, and it will help you with generating support for any changes you might want to make once you see the data.

"I'll get started on that ASAP, first thing tomorrow," Jerry states excitedly, feeling like forward action will help with closing the gaps he's just beginning to realize exist on top of the gaps he knows about already.

"Great, I look forward to hearing about it," Cuthbert states. They agree to meet again in a week.

SHOW ME THE NUMBERS

The parking lot is largely empty as Jerry arrives at the office earlier than normal, still energized from his conversation with Cuthbert the night before. He had preset the coffee maker for Haley as he left before dawn, despite the late evening, but now he needs his morning jolt of caffeine. The Cons office has a small cafeteria, so Jerry walks over to grab a coffee.

Coffee in hand, he passes Cameron's office. To his surprise, Cameron is at his desk—he normally does not show up before nine. Even more surprising, when Cameron catches sight of Jerry walking past, he jumps up and calls out, "Hey, Jerry, do you have a minute?"

As Jerry sits down, Cameron exclaims, "Jerry, we need to talk employee engagement. The results are in, and they are not good. Overall, for the company, engagement has dropped by nearly 5 percent compared to last year. We in Client Services are down 6 percent; your team is down by 5.5 percent. Gordon is irate and wants us to propose an action plan. Do you have some time to work on that with me this week?"

Jerry protests. "Cameron, I wish I could help, but we are completely underwater, I am three people short, and Bellamy is on my case. Is this really that urgent?"

Cameron looks annoyed. "Well, Jerry, I am sorry, but I have to insist. Employees are the foundation of Cons' success, and I don't think we should delay taking action. By the way, you are also behind on your performance reviews. I will email you a copy of the survey results, and I am looking forward to your thoughts. I will set up a meeting for us later this week."

Jerry leaves Cameron's office feeling a bit deflated. Once in his own office, he updates his whiteboard.

- FILL 2̶ 3 OPEN POSITIONS
- TEAM PERFORMANCE REVIEWS
- SERVICE ISSUE UPDATE FOR MONDAY SALES MEETING
- ~~FIX 80 LIFE CASES~~
- CREATE WORK INVENTORY
- EMPLOYEE ENGAGEMENT SURVEY RESPONSE

Jerry decides that, amid this sea of urgencies, taking inventory of the work in his department nevertheless should be done right away. Maybe Cuthbert was right, and not everything his department did was necessary or at least connected to a client need. Hey, it was worth a try. Cuthbert had suggested creating a team and gathering data points. But who should be on it? Mary and Johnny, for sure—as seasoned supervisors they knew the process inside out. But what about those doing the actual work? From Julia's team, Ryan seemed the most open-minded. Olivia undoubtedly understood the work, so Jerry decides to ask her to represent Johnny's group. And for Mary's team, Michele is the obvious choice. As he is getting ready to compose an email inviting them all to a meeting to explain what needed to get done, he is interrupted by a knock at his door.

"Are we still meeting for our weekly touch base?" It is Hannah, who has popped her head into his office. As he looks up, he sees Ryan, Lee, and Eric standing behind her and suddenly realizes that he completely forgot about the weekly meeting he had scheduled with Julia's team.

Jerry nods. "Of course! Sorry, I lost track of time. Let's grab the conference room."

The flipchart from last week's staff meeting is still on the wall.

Settling into his chair, Jerry realizes that this is a perfect opportunity to get started on his assignment for Cuthbert. "I was wondering if you all could walk me through the work you are doing. Since I'm going to be filling in as your supervisor until we find a replacement for Julia, I think I need to get a better understanding of what you all do." Looking at their faces, he could see they were confused. "So, if you don't mind, maybe each one of you could walk me through what you do in a typical week?"

After a moment of silence, Ryan speaks up. "Well, Lee and I are mostly working on putting together the implementation package for each case, which includes issuing the order for printing ID cards and preparing employee communications— for the online guidelines or printed handbooks."

"Is there anything else you two do?"

Lee jumps in. "Well, let's see . . . we also update the case tracker, respond to status update requests from Sales, and process census changes."

Hannah chimes in. "I am responsible for creating the coverage certificate and the first bill. And, of course, I have to deal with Customer Service all the time, when clients complain about incorrect bills and certificates—which is, by the way, mostly the client's fault. If they would give us correct data in the first place, we wouldn't have so many issues."

Jerry nods. "So, what about you, Eric?"

Eric stares at him. "Well, I am responsible for quality control, so I check every document before we send it to the client. Oh, and I manage the quality scorecard."

Jerry stands up and starts capturing what he heard on the flipchart:

- Prepare implementation package

- Print ID cards

- Prepare communications

- Update case tracker

- Create coverage certificate

- Create first bill

- Respond to Customer Service issues

- Provide sales updates

- Process census changes

- Review documents to ensure quality

- Maintain quality scorecard

"Is that everything?"

Ryan raises his hand. "Well, we also create the sales forecast." Jerry adds the sales forecast to the list. "Anything else?"

Eric grins. "What about this meeting and our monthly staff meeting?"

Jerry ponders that for a second. "You're absolutely right, Eric. Let's add that, too. Is that all?"

Hannah chimes in once more. "We are forgetting about Julia's work. She assigns the work to us and does the secondary review. And we did not include any trainings."

The team nods. Jerry updates the list and is now eager to move on. "So could you estimate how much of your time goes against each of these tasks?" The team seems perplexed. "What I mean is how many hours do you think you spend on doing each of these tasks each month?"

After a lengthy discussion and much back and forth, the team works its way through the list and for each task arrives at an estimate of the time required. They assume everybody works two thousand hours each year, and they decide to factor in the open supervisor position, such that their total capacity comes to ten thousand hours. After going through the list several times and adjusting the numbers rigorously to add up to the total time available—and with no shortage of spirited cajoling—everybody eventually agrees that their estimates are directionally correct.

TASK	HOURS/YEAR	PERCENTAGE
Prepare implementation package	1,600	16%
Print ID cards	1,500	15%
Prepare communications	200	2%
Update case tracker	200	2%

continued

Create coverage certificate	800	8%
Create first bill	800	8%
Respond to Customer Service issues	500	5%
Create sales forecast	300	3%
Process census changes	400	4%
Review documents to ensure quality	1,500	15%
Maintain quality scorecard	300	3%
Provide sales updates	400	4%
Meetings	300	3%
Assign caseload	800	8%
Secondary quality review	200	2%
Trainings	100	1%
Other (performance reviews, etc.)	100	1%
Total	10,000	100%

"Looks like we are spending a lot of time on things that have nothing to do with moving the case forward, such as the sales forecast," observes Ryan.

Jerry nods thoughtfully. "Yes, I think that is very interesting."

Hannah observes, "And we spend a lot of time on quality checks."

Jerry agrees. "I hope we can find a way to get rid of some of that work, so we can spend more time on the real work." He adds, "Just so you all know, I'm going to ask Mary and Johnny to do this very same thing, to create a task list for their teams."

He glances at his watch. Only five minutes left. *Well, this has been a very productive meeting*, he thinks. He asks the team to help manage the caseload assignment themselves, until a replacement for Julia has been found. They all readily agree, and Jerry feels a sense of relief. Looking again at his watch, Jerry realizes that he is already running late for his next meeting. They agree to meet again next week. As they file out of the room, Jerry remembers the performance reviews. "Oh, and keep an eye out for a meeting invite to do your annual performance review—we need to get those done ASAP."

Energized by the discussion, he shares the analysis they did for Julia's team right away with Mary and Johnny. "Makes a lot of sense to challenge some of this," says Johnny.

Mary agrees. "If we can get rid of some of this work somehow, it will help us catch up."

"Great, can you do the same exercise with your teams?" Jerry asks, seizing the opportunity to also get their buy-in for the team Cuthbert suggested. "I would like to form a team that takes a close look at our work and enable us to come up with a better way of doing things. What do you think?"

Mary is the first to respond. "Not a bad idea, but who should be on that team?"

"I was thinking both of you, of course, plus one member from each of your teams. Who would you recommend?"

When Mary and Johnny suggest Michele and Olivia, he quickly agrees. *Great minds think alike*, thinks Jerry. Michele's keen knack for embracing what's possible—for thinking creatively out of the box—will be the perfect complement to Olivia's extensive experience and Ryan's open-mindedness and solid pragmatism.

They align to have the kick-off meeting for the team the following week.

Feeling accomplished enough for the day and eager for his next meeting with Cuthbert in the coming week, Jerry heads home.

SCRAPING THE BARREL

Bob had come through. Well, at least he had lined up a few candidates for the two open roles on Jerry's team. Four candidates, to be exact. And he had scheduled all the interviews for tomorrow. Yet, as positive as that might be, *there goes my day*, thinks Jerry. He had hoped to finally tackle the performance reviews for Julia's team this week, but that would have to wait.

Jerry quickly glances at the resumes, and at least on paper they all look suitable. With a little luck he might be able to fill at least one of the open roles. Jerry considers asking Johnny and Mary to join him for the interviews, but a look at their calendars for the next day reveals both are tied up with other work.

Arriving early to accommodate the additions to his calendar, Jerry prepares to meet Meredith, the first candidate. She did her undergraduate at Georgia State (*Well, not everybody is perfect*, Jerry thinks, in jest, of course). After college, she worked for two years for a clinical research organization, enrolling candidates in clinical trials—a job that requires attention to detail. The open position in Mary's group happens to be the one to which Meredith has applied. It could be a good fit, Jerry surmises.

The interview goes well, at least up to the point when Jerry describes the actual work Meredith would do. He senses she starts losing interest when he explains the need to follow up on cases that are missing some information.

Jerry pauses and looks at her. "So, Meredith, what questions do you have?"

She glances at him. "Well, the job sounds fairly simple. So, what are the opportunities to progress?"

Jerry smiles. "Well, if all goes well, once you've gained some experience with us, I would think that you could move up to a supervisory position, assuming a position opens up."

Meredith nods. "Well, I like the idea of working with clients, so that is appealing, although . . ." Her voice trails off, as though she was about to say something further but decided better of it.

"Well, actually, you will be working mostly with Sales—they're responsible for working with the brokers and asking them to reach out to the clients, if there are issues to address—" Jerry halts abruptly, as he realizes, after hearing himself say it, how disappointingly dull that must sound. But it's too late.

Judging from her body language, she is losing all interest in the role. "So it's mainly inputting data into the computer system and working with the Sales department to set up new client cases or files. Is that correct?" she asks.

My God, Jerry thinks, *when you put it like that* . . . Doing his level best to remain undaunted, Jerry tries hard for the next ten minutes to make the job sound important, citing how crucial their benefits packages are to the thousands of employees employed by Consolidated's corporate clients. But he senses to his own horror that this too sounds hollow and vaguely unfulfilling, as he watches Meredith's eyes glaze over.

At the end of the interview, they shake hands, and as he walks her to the conference room door, Jerry mutters, "Well, we have a couple of candidates for this role, but we will get back to you in a few days if we decide we want to proceed." She smiles politely, but Jerry can tell she is not interested in the role.

Fifteen minutes before the next interview, Jerry sits down and looks at Meredith's resume again, jotting down some observations from their less-than-spectacular meeting. But his mind drifts back to his conversation with Cuthbert. It was rather clear that she is not interested in the role. Or if she had been interested when she first walked in, she certainly seemed less so by the time the interview was over. But why?

Suddenly, Jerry remembers Cuthbert's definition of a good job: "meaningful work, autonomy, and feedback."

He performs a quick analysis in his head: not a lot of variety, if he is being honest. Responsibility for the entire work product? No. Important to others? In a way, yes—if his department messes up, their systems would have the wrong information. Then that incorrect information would lead to problems later on when claims are processed. And, of course, the billing would be off. And that certainly would lead to complaints later as well. So not the kind of "important to others" that a job candidate would be looking for. And then autonomy. Thinking from the perspective of a candidate like Meredith, there is not a whole lot. And what about feedback?

A knock at the door interrupts his thoughts. The next candidate is waiting for him, a young man. Jerry ushers him in.

After this interview, Jerry's mood turns sour once again, a state that is becoming all too constant. None of the candidates seemed very excited about the jobs they were interviewing for.

And he is starting to see more clearly why. Yes, the work of his department is important, but important to whom? Important to Consolidated's Claims and Customer Service and Billing departments? Of course. Vitally important to the client companies and their covered employees? Certainly. But important to the people on his team? Maybe not so much. How on earth can his team know and understand how important their work is to the client companies and the employees they serve, if in fact they never talk directly to those clients? Jerry conjures a vision of his team sitting in a huge black box, passing paper documents through slits in the wall to the outside world.

Indeed, if Jerry looks closely at the patterns, he has to admit Cuthbert is right. These jobs are hard to sell. But then Jerry goes deeper into it, as if he's channeling Cuthbert's words: These jobs *as they are presently designed and structured* are hard to sell. Bottom line: The jobs do not measure up to Cuthbert's model of what a "good job" actually is.

Bob does not even knock—he just waltzes into Jerry's office. "How did it go? Anybody you liked?"

Jerry grimaces. "Bob, I am not sure any one of them is really interested in the job."

Bob looks at him. "What do you mean? What is there not to like? We offer a good health insurance plan, we have a 401(k) with matching, and the salary is not bad for an entry-level role."

Jerry nods. "I don't think it's the pay or the benefits, Bob. They all asked about opportunities to advance, but, of course, that is somewhat limited. It seems they all were looking for something more meaningful."

Bob looks at him somewhat incredulously. "Meaningful? Geez Louise. What is wrong with a steady paycheck? Well, let me know what you want to do. Anybody you want us to follow up with and make an offer?"

Jerry thinks for a second. Well, he needs to fill the open positions. And at least two of the candidates seemed qualified. Meredith, the first candidate, certainly can do the job. Walter, the last candidate, also impressed him. Walter had clearly done his homework on Cons, although he possessed little work experience.

The other two candidates had been underwhelming: Valerie had clearly not understood what the job entailed, and Caspar, who admittedly did not want to be there, had irritated Jerry by chewing gum during the entire interview. But beggars can't be choosers, as Jerry's dad had always told him. He urgently needs to get some help.

"Well, let's make an offer to Meredith and Walter. Can we offer a sign-on bonus to sweeten the pie?"

Bob sighs. "Well, I hate to do that, but if it helps, okay, I'll offer two grand. That should help pay those pesky student loans. You sure you want to move ahead with these two?"

Jerry nods. If he could fill the two open positions, it would help tackle the mountain of cases. And maybe the improvement work he has started with the team will help make the jobs more interesting, once the new hires are on board.

Bob smiles. "Okay, Jerry, I will get on that straightaway. Oh, and by the way, you need to open a requisition for Julia's role—assuming you want to fill it."

Confused by the comment, Jerry asks, "Why do I need to create a requisition? Julia left, so there is an open role."

"Well, that is technically true," Bob replies, "but as of the start of this year, Finance is asking us to re-justify any open role, just in case it is not needed."

Jerry feels his blood pressure rising. "We are drowning in open cases, I have Sales breathing down my neck, and Finance wants to check whether we really need the head count? That is ridiculous!"

Bob sighs. "Jerry, you are not the only one complaining, but you also know that the company is under a lot of pressure. Profits have been going down for three quarters now, and something has to give."

Jerry takes a breath, realizing that Bob is only the messenger. *Clearly, the folks in Finance need to get their heads examined*, Jerry thinks. "Fine," he relents. "I will put together a requisition."

"Excellent. Get that to me ASAP, so I can put it through the process. In the meantime, let me put together these offers."

Bob leaves, and Jerry looks at the clock. It's 6:00 p.m. Time to get going. He grabs his phone, closes his office door, braces for the inevitable traffic, and heads home.

As he sits down for dinner with Haley, she can tell his mind is still at the office. "What's wrong?"

Jerry shares with Haley details about his day. He describes the brutal details of the four interviews, and his conversation with Bob. "Haley, if I am frank with you, the jobs these kids interviewed for are really not that interesting, at least not on the surface. If I am honest with myself, I probably would have taken either job when I finished college, but it seems that this new generation is looking for something else. And I don't blame them."

Haley nods sympathetically. "Well, what can you do about that?"

Jerry nods. "Not a darn thing." But as the words come out of his mouth, he realizes that he can do something about that. By explaining to him what made for a good job, Cuthbert had given him a recipe: a formula for creating an interesting, meaningful job. His mind races.

After they finish their meal, Jerry excuses himself. "You gave me a good idea. I think I need an hour to think about that a bit more."

Haley smiles. "Well, you go sort out your work problems. I'll be downstairs catching up on my *Sex in the City* reruns."

Jerry grimaces. He dislikes that show.

After helping Haley clear the table, he heads up to his little office tucked in the attic. He had worked from home during the first couple months of the pandemic. But the company had asked everybody to get back to the office shortly after the last wave receded. There had been some protests, but they had died down quickly. And while he hated his commute, Jerry had been mostly happy to go back to the office—he had missed the in-person interactions with his team.

Sitting in his attic office, Jerry goes over Cuthbert's list. Doing the work from start to finish and being responsible for the entire work product. *Are those things even possible?* he ponders. He goes through the entire process in his head. Well, in theory, one person could do it all, but that would require a lot of training. It would certainly provide more variety, though. *And be more interesting*, Jerry thinks.

It is close to midnight as he crawls into bed next to Haley. She is half asleep but mumbles, "Did you solve all your problems?" He smiles. "Not yet, honey," he whispers, "but I have some ideas. Sleep tight."

HOT POTATOES

J erry hates performance reviews—both getting them and giving them. And today it is time to give them. He had been dragging them out for a couple of weeks now, but he is running out of time—if he does not get them into the system before the close of the quarter, he won't get his own bonus. And this year he needs to do reviews not only for his supervisors but also for Julia's entire team, and of course he has no idea how to judge their performance.

He has been looking at the productivity reports Mary is pulling together for the entire department, but they are not very helpful in judging performance. In theory, he should be able to judge them by how many cases they completed, but cases could be so different—the time needed to do the work is always so dependent on how thoroughly the client responds to their information requests, and the coverage they have bought is always different. Mary recently added a quality score, but it was impossible to trace back to where the problem had originated and who had screwed up, as problems often were only detected when the client went live. He wishes he had asked Julia to do the reviews before she left or at least leave him some notes, but he had been too busy putting out fires.

And being a glutton for punishment, he had scheduled all four of them on the same day. When would he ever learn?

As he gets ready for the first review with Ryan, he keeps thinking about Cuthbert's "good job" concept. He has been wondering whether his employees actually cared about any of that. Since he did not really have that much to say about their performance, maybe that is something he should explore during the conversation?

Just then, Ryan knocks at the door. "Good time to chat?" Jerry waves him in. "Yes, of course. Let's do it." For most of the conversation, Jerry follows the script HR had sent him back in January: Review projects against goals and accomplishments, identify development needs, explore the employee's aspirations, agree on goals for the next year, and ask for feedback as a manager.

Ryan is well prepared and starts the discussion by handing him a copy of his goals for the previous year, annotated with what he had accomplished: Learn how to handle more complex cases. But as they move on to talking about aspirations, Jerry asks Ryan where he sees himself in five years.

Ryan struggles to answer the question. "To be honest, Jerry, I don't know what my aspiration should be. I am now comfortable dealing with the more complex cases—Julia gave me a couple of tough nuts to crack, which was good. It was challenging. But I am not sure what comes next. It seems the only way forward is to become a supervisor, and I don't think I am ready for that."

Jerry nods. Ryan has a point. Where are the opportunities to develop? He decides to switch gears—and take a gamble. "Ryan, what do you think about the job itself? How meaningful is the work to you?"

Ryan is quiet for a few seconds. "Permission to be frank, Jerry?"

Jerry laughs. "Permission granted."

Ryan hesitates for a second. "Not a lot. I mean, I understand why we do what we do. Of course, it is important to get the clients set up correctly, but our group is sitting at the end of the process. We are so dependent on what the other teams are doing, and since we are the last group, we always get screwed when their timelines slip. And then we end up juggling all the hot potatoes. Julia tried to support as much as she could, but the priorities are changing all the time. And it just feels like a constant onslaught of tasks. We try to do the best we can, but in most cases, the ship has already sailed. The census keeps changing all the time, so you never get to finish anything you started. And billing is a real bear!"

Jerry tries to be empathetic. "Yes, I can understand that. So it sounds like you feel you have little control over what you need to do?"

Ryan cannot suppress a chuckle. "Control is an illusion, Jerry. Especially in this job!"

Jerry continues, "But what about feedback? How can you tell whether you are doing a good job?"

"Well, Julia has been doing one-on-ones, and during those meetings she always reviewed our quality scores. And in recent months we also started to look at the customer service issues, but those often trace back to what happened months ago. Sometimes it was not even me who screwed up. I mean, I feel like I do the best I can. But I really don't have any real data to back that up."

Wow, Cuthbert was right, Jerry thinks. "Ryan, thanks for being so honest."

Ryan smiles.

Jerry presses on. "Now, going back to goals for this year, I was wondering if it would be okay with you if we keep that generic for the time being. I have some ideas for changing how we organize the work, but it's still in the early stages."

"Sure," Ryan says, "that sounds fine. And no problem, Jerry. I understand." Ryan begins to rise to his feet, but Jerry stops him with a gesture of his hand.

"Actually, there's one more thing. I'm forming an exploratory team to really take a hard, no-holds-barred look at how we do things around here—everything from workflows to task management—to see if we can't design a better way of doing things." Jerry pauses and then adds, "I'd like you to be on that team."

Ryan sits stone-faced, staring, it seems, at the back of Jerry's neck. "I'm in," he says.

"Great. And thanks for all the good work you are doing."

Lee is next. He is less prepared than Ryan. When Jerry pulls up the previous year's objectives, it seems as if Lee has never seen them before. Even before Jerry asks, Lee exclaims that he is not interested in becoming a supervisor—ever. "I saw all the nonsense Julia had to deal with," he offers. "I just want to be part of a winning team. Unlike the Braves!"

But when Jerry asks him whether he thinks they are winning, Lee becomes quiet.

"Jerry, to be honest, that is hard to tell. I mean, we have these little victories, when we manage to get a client set up on the system just in time. But then we hear a couple of months later that the client is pissed off for some bogus reason. And the bills,

Jerry, the bills are never right. I mean, I just sent the ninth revision of BQA's bill to the National Accounts team. I'm sure I will do the tenth one soon."

Again, Jerry has to admit Cuthbert is right. And Lee has a point, too. People want to be part of a winning team—and have at least a chance to win. But what did winning look like for the onboarding department? And could any of them really make a difference? *You can only do a good job if there is a good job to be done.* So true.

They wrap up the conversation, and just as Ryan was, Lee is also okay with keeping the objectives very high level. Jerry is grateful—it will make it easier to fill out the ridiculous template the HR folks have obliged him to use.

Hannah is next. Jerry has been dreading the conversation with her, knowing she will likely be pushing to be promoted to Julia's old role.

And Hannah does not surprise. She starts out with an elaborate presentation of her various accomplishments, all of which are pretty vague and a little embellished as well, Jerry surmises. When the conversation moves on to her longer-term aspirations, Hannah immediately proclaims her desire to become a supervisor. And now with Julia gone, she is wondering—"inquiring," she says—about the position. "I think I'm qualified."

Jerry is able to stop her before she can launch into a full-blown stump speech.

"Hannah, we will post that position as soon as it is approved, and then you—or anybody else within Cons who thinks they are qualified—can throw their hat in the ring. But I am also thinking about making some changes to the way we work. I mean, you know about our backlog challenge. And for the time being I need you to be patient, keep up the good work, and help us clear the backlog."

Hannah is clearly not happy about that answer. "But Jerry, how about you just make me the interim supervisor?"

Jerry is stunned by her persistence. "Hannah, I am sorry, but I cannot make that commitment right now. But I can promise you that one of my objectives is to make the work more interesting. Give me some time, please."

Hannah grudgingly agrees, and she also accepts Jerry's proposal to keep the objectives for this year very high level. But when Jerry asks her whether she feels part of a winning team and encourages her to speak freely, the expression on her face speaks volumes. Jerry can see the defeat in her eyes.

"Winning?" Hannah retorts. "We are in a race to shovel manure from one place to another, Jerry. Give me a break!"

Jerry wraps up the discussion before Hannah is able to expand on that statement. He already knows what will come next.

Three down, one more to go. Jerry works over lunch to update the dreaded HR system, wolfing down some leftover pasta he found in the fridge at home. The final performance review of the day is Eric. Eric, the mystery man.

The conversation follows the same pattern. Eric is somewhat prepared. He ticks off his accomplishments. But when it comes to the question about where he sees himself in five years, Eric leans forward. "Jerry, you are a nice guy. I don't know how you manage to be so positive, given the amount of crap you have to deal with. But this job stinks. It always has; it always will. Sales dumps their dirty laundry off, and we do the best we can, but"— he pauses for dramatic effect—"if it quacks like a duck and it walks like a duck, it's a duck!"

Jerry cannot suppress a grin. This is already the most expansive conversation he has had with Eric, and he cannot help but admit that he likes his candor. "But Eric, don't you think we can—"

"Change that?" Eric interrupts, almost derisively. "No, not at all."

Jerry gets the message. And he saves himself from asking Eric about meaningful work, autonomy, and feedback. As with the others, he explains that he wants to make some changes and asks Eric if it would be okay to keep the objectives a bit high level.

"No problem, Jerry. And just for the record, I am rooting for you. But I don't think we can win."

After Eric leaves his office, Jerry reflects on what he has learned. Clearly, everybody on Julia's former team hates their job. And he can't blame them.

Lee had a point: Everybody wants to be part of a winning team. And if he puts himself in their shoes, he cannot see a path to win. They are doing little bits and pieces, the technology is broken, priorities constantly shift, and they have no real connection to the client. What does winning look like in a setup like that? Jerry decides to call it a day and heads home.

Just as Jerry is sitting down for dinner with Haley that Thursday night, his phone lets him know that he has a new email from Mary titled "What we do all day." He grimaces but puts the phone away just as Haley walks into the room carrying their plates.

"How is your girlfriend?"

Surprised, he looks at Haley and then realizes she is pulling his leg. "You got me there, hon," he proclaims, playing along. "Mary and her dirty thoughts . . ." He realizes quickly that he took the joke too far and pulls out his phone. "Here, check out the sexy messages she is sending me."

He hands her his phone, suddenly hoping as he does so that the email Mary sent is indeed work related. Now, thinking of it, he realizes that the subject line was a bit strange.

Haley looks at his phone, taps open Mary's message, and laughs. "Is this what y'all call work?" She hands the phone back.

He looks at the screen. Mary's email is terse: "Jerry, Johnny and I sat down with our respective teams, and here is how we as a department spend our time. Let's talk!" He opens the attached document. It takes him a second to make sense of the chart.

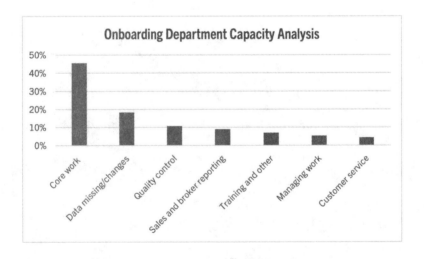

This can't be right, Jerry thinks, shaking his head. *We are spending less than half our time doing the actual case work.* He replies with a quick text of his own, asking Mary to set up a meeting for the three of them to review the numbers. And Mary being Mary, his phone alerts him to a meeting invite, for the next day at 4:00 p.m., before he even finishes his meal. *She needs to get a life*, Jerry wryly thinks, but then he corrects his thinking: *We all need to get a life.*

TGIF

"**J**erry, this is Elrod. I heard about the RPA business going on and would like to talk with you to limit the damage of this little stunt. Please call me back."

Jerry listens to Elrod's voicemail twice. Stunt? Damage? This is not what Jerry wants to deal with on top of everything else. And that adversarial tone is troubling, even demeaning.

When Johnny and Mary file into his office at 4:00 p.m., Jerry is dead tired. And as much as he would like to blow off the meeting and head home, his curiosity has got the better of him. Mary and Johnny walk him through the data behind the chart Mary shared, using a humongous spreadsheet listing all the work done in the department. From what he can initially surmise, it seems to capture everything they do. "Very impressive, gang. So . . . what do we make out of all this?"

Johnny grins. "Well, not sure, boss. The missing data is clearly out of our control, and I don't think there is anything we can do."

Mary chimes in. "And we definitely need quality checks—otherwise it is garbage in, garbage out."

Hard to disagree with that, thinks Jerry. "Okay, but what about the sales reporting? I cannot believe we spend that much time on that."

"I agree with you, Jerry, but I am not sure we are in a good position to get into a fight with Sales right now," Johnny says. *He has a point*, Jerry thinks.

They review the remainder of the chart. *Not much there*, Jerry observes, but he says nothing, continuing to ponder: *We need training, the team needs to be managed, and dealing with Customer Service is part of the job. With Sales being already unhappy, pushing back on reporting might just be the straw that breaks the camel's back.*

And on top of all of that, he still has to deal with Elrod. Well, not today. He makes a mental note to reach out to him next week, hoping whatever issue is brewing there will at least keep for the time being.

10

THE GIFT

After a weekend that seemed to go by extra-quickly, Jerry readies for his early Monday morning meeting with Cuthbert. They had decided to meet at a coffee shop near an outdoor mall, a place notably quiet this early in the day. As Jerry arrives, he sees Cuthbert picking up his coffee at the counter and making his way to a corner table.

"Good weekend, Jerry?"

"Yes. Busy Saturday and slower Sunday, which was nice," Jerry replies. "Just went by too fast! But on the work front, we made some good progress last week, and I'm eager to share."

"Let's get to it!" Cuthbert encourages.

They review the analysis. "What shocked me the most was that only 45 percent of our time is focused on what my team calls core work," Jerry explains. "And how much time we spend checking the quality of our work. But we cannot compromise on quality. We can't do anything about the missing data. And while we clearly spend a lot of time on sales reporting, I see little opportunity here."

Cuthbert smiles. "I disagree somewhat, Jerry. I think you might be able to free up some time here. You get reports too, right?"

Jerry nods. "Sure. A ton."

"Which ones do you use the most?"

Jerry sighs. "The weekly priority list. It tells us which cases we should prioritize, and it comes directly from Sales. Let's see, the customer service statistics, the monthly budget update—"

Cuthbert gently interrupts. "Those all sound very important. Do you also get reports you don't need or where you just need a few numbers?"

Jerry nods. "The weekly productivity reports for each of the teams. Each team member tracks their time against the case, but it doesn't really tell me anything. Each case is different, and sometimes a small case takes twice as much time as a large client implementation. It all depends on the actual products we sold and how quickly—and how thoroughly—they respond to our requests, and so on."

Cuthbert smiles. "So, what do you actually do with it?"

Jerry is now clearly embarrassed. "Well, I file it in case I need to go back to it at some time."

Now Cuthbert grins ear to ear. "Well, I am sure not too much effort goes into producing this report?"

"Well, it should not be more than ten or fifteen minutes per person each day, and then some time for Mary to pull it all together." As Jerry listens to himself speak, he starts doing the math in his head: *15 people × 15 minutes × 5 days × 50 weeks + 50 × however long it took Mary . . .*

But before he could finish the calculation, Cuthbert says, "Give or take a thousand hours or half a person."

Jerry is stunned. Producing that report took half of somebody's time—and he did not do anything with it.

Cuthbert smiles. "Don't feel bad, Jerry. But you could call this non-value-added. And if you are looking to free up time, you should get rid of it. And maybe—just maybe—you want to check whether your internal customers need all those other reports your team produces. Maybe they don't need them at all, or maybe they just need a few pieces of data. It never hurts to check."

Although Jerry has doubts this will help free up a lot of time, he agrees to investigate. "It will be interesting to see if we can streamline some of that. If we can get rid of at least some of this, it will certainly help. But what about the core work?"

Cuthbert laughs. "Spot on, Jerry. That is of course the most important part. But by minimizing the work that does not add much value, you free up capacity—and right now it looks like you will need plenty of that. For the core work, the first part of this is to understand how the work gets done today—and who does it. Are you familiar with process mapping?"

Jerry nods.

"Great," Cuthbert continues, "I would suggest you use your first team meeting to get everybody aligned on the current state. A swim lane chart that shows who does what is probably the most suitable way to capture that. Do you know what that is?"

"Yes—you create a swim lane for each department, so you can see who does what," Jerry replies.

"Exactly. It will help you identify the handoffs between groups," Cuthbert says. "Try to be as granular as you can. Ideally, you walk from station to station so that everybody understands the entire flow, and once the team is aligned on the current state, you can start thinking about how it *should* be, the future state. Jerry, are you familiar with the concept of 'definition of done'?"

Jerry nods. "Yes, that is part of Agile, right?"

"Correct. Definition of done is an agreement among the

design team as to what done looks like. So, with that in mind, here is what I would suggest you use as your definition of done for a well-designed job." He pulls out a well-worn index card and hands it to Jerry.

Jerry peruses the card.

- I HAVE ALMOST COMPLETE RESPONSIBILITY FOR DECIDING HOW AND WHEN THE WORK IS TO BE DONE.
- JUST DOING THE WORK PROVIDES ME WITH OPPORTUNITIES TO FIGURE OUT HOW WELL I AM DOING.
- I DO A COMPLETE TASK FROM START TO FINISH. THE RESULTS OF MY EFFORTS ARE CLEARLY VISIBLE AND IDENTIFIABLE.
- I HAVE THE OPPORTUNITY TO DO A NUMBER OF DIFFERENT TASKS, USING A WIDE VARIETY OF SKILLS AND TALENTS.
- WHAT I DO AFFECTS OTHERS IN VERY IMPORTANT WAYS.
- THE TECHNOLOGY I USE TO PERFORM MY WORK IS WELL DESIGNED AND MAKES THE JOB EASIER.

Cuthbert explains, "Define the work in a way that once you are done your employees would fully agree with these statements. You can keep it—use these as your design principles."

Jerry reads the card again, this time with the feeling he's received a gift of a sort that will yield dividends—to what extent he does not yet comprehend.

11

KILLING COWS

The first meeting of the special team starts promptly at 9:00 a.m., with Jerry explaining the purpose of the group. "As you all know, we are in a bit of a pickle. Our backlog of open cases has more than doubled from where we were a year ago, and with three open roles, we are destined to fall even further behind, unless we do something."

He looks around the table. "Even if we could fill the open slots today, it would take months for them to come up to speed, so that would not help us in the near term. So, I would like this team to challenge how we work and see if we can find a way to be more productive."

Ryan raises his hand. "Yes, Ryan?"

"What do you mean by more productive?" he asks.

Jerry smiles. "Ryan, great question. You remember the activity analysis we did, where we looked at what we do and how much of our capacity, meaning time, it consumes?"

Ryan nods. "Yes, of course."

"Okay, we did this for the entire department. And here is what we found."

Jerry shares the summary Mary put together. He points at

the bar on the chart labeled "core work." "It looks like we spend less than half our time on core work—getting the information into the system so that everything downstream works. We need to free up time spent on noncritical stuff to make a dent into our backlog, otherwise the backlog will grow, more and more cases will go live without data in the system, and then Claims and Customer Service will suffer, and of course Sales will be on our backs because the brokers are upset because the clients are pissed off because their members run into problems when they file claims."

Jerry pauses. "Hmm, what I want us to do is rethink how we do our work, see if we can be more efficient, and stop doing stuff that does not add value."

Olivia jumps in. "What do you mean by stuff that doesn't add value?" Jerry points at the bar labeled "managing work."

"Let me give you an example," he offers. "You all are familiar with the productivity report, right? Well, that is an example of work that is non-value-added. I am the customer for that particular report—the guy the report is generated for—and I may be the only customer for that particular report. You all record your time, Mary crunches the numbers and creates a comprehensive report, but," Jerry pauses, feeling a bit embarrassed, "I actually don't do anything with that information."

Mary leans forward. "What do you mean, Jerry? It takes me two hours each week to put the whole thing together."

"Yes, Mary, I know how much of a time sucker it is. But you all know that each case is different, so the report actually tells me nothing actionable, so I end up just filing it."

From the look on Mary's face, he can tell he has struck a nerve. "I feel really bad about this, but it is a good example for us needing to look at everything we do and really question it. We need to focus our limited capacity on getting these cases through the process, and we need to challenge anything that does not directly tie to that—anything that does not advance our core work. No sacred cows. Every small change will help."

Michele perks up. "Does that mean no more time tracking? Yes!"

Jerry nods. "Yes, no more time tracking—at least until we can figure out a way to collect information that helps make decisions. And, Mary, I am really sorry for not realizing this sooner. Mea culpa."

Jerry points at the bar labeled "sales and broker reporting. "I think we should take a hard look at all those sales reports and find out what our friends in Sales are doing with that information. If we can cut back on all that effort that is not tied to the core mission of our department, hopefully we can free up some time we can reinvest in what really matters. What do you all think?"

Everybody nods approvingly. And it looks like even Mary, who seemed a bit shaken when he labeled her report as non-value-added, is back on board—she volunteers to investigate whether Sales really needs all those reports. Jerry asks her to keep a low profile—no need to aggravate an already tense relationship.

With that out of the way, he explains to the team that he wants to map the process. They have a lively discussion about where to start and in the end agree that the process starts with the signed contract. "That is when the clock starts ticking," is how Jerry puts it, and nobody objects. By the end of the meeting, the walls of the conference room are covered with sticky notes.

When they are done, Jerry asks the group for their thoughts.

Client	Contract signed	Data request						
Broker	Submit contract							
Sales	Log contract							
Prep	Receive contract	Log in system	Estimate workload	Assign to associate	Review client document	Request missing info	Assemble package	Quality check
Setup	Receive package	Assign to associate	Enter data into system	Quality check				
Bill	Assemble package	Create coverage certificate	Create first bill	Quality check				

Johnny is the first one to chime in. "We sure do a lot of checking everywhere."

Michele agrees. "And we still find problems at the very end of the process."

Mary jumps in. "Plus, remember that we decided a while back that for the cases on the priority list, my team hands the case over to Johnny's group after ten days, even if the client has not provided all the missing information."

"And that creates a ton of problems for us, Mary," exclaims Johnny, "so maybe we need to rethink that."

Jerry is mindful of the time. "Gang, we only have a few minutes left, but this is a great start. We probably should share this with the rest of the crew at our next departmental meeting."

He pauses. Should he mention the "good job" concept Cuthbert introduced him to? *Too soon*, he thinks. "Really taking a hard look at what we do and how we can do it better will take a bit of time," Jerry acknowledges. "This process map is really just the beginning. If you all are okay with it, I will schedule a few more sessions for us to really dig into this. I promise you it will be worth your time."

They further agree to use the next few days to socialize the map with their colleagues. Jerry closes by stating, "This was a very insightful and productive meeting. Let's meet again next week, and let's see how we take this forward."

Ryan raises his hand.

"Yes, Ryan?"

"Well, if we are now a team working on this, maybe we should have a name?"

Johnny laughs out loud.

"Great idea, Ryan. Anybody have a good idea for what we should call ourselves?"

Ryan grins. "What about Cow Killers? Like in 'killing the sacred cows'?"

The room erupts in laughter. "That's it—Cow Killers," Jerry pronounces. "A bit politically incorrect, but I like it. But please—don't go printing any T-shirts with that name!"

And with that, the Cow Killer team is born.

Later that day, Mary knocks on Jerry's open door. He motions her in.

"Trouble with Northpoint Solutions again," Mary starts. "We missed the initial deadline. Michele and Rasheed are working overtime, but the system update to reconcile has been delayed by IT. So we are in a holding pattern and can't even give them a reliable ETA. They are not happy, Jerry, and I'm concerned. We are understaffed, as you know, and I can't keep asking the team for more hours. We are really trying to do what's right for the client here!"

"I know, and you're right. I appreciate your bringing this to me," Jerry affirms. "I'll see if I can get a better ETA from IT. We can't leave our clients with uncertain timing—especially since we don't have the best track record with Northpoint."

Not the best track record is an understatement, they both abundantly know. Northpoint Solutions had been a Cons client years ago, but Cons had lost the business when, because of a glitch in Cons' claims management system, all claims were automatically rejected—which nobody noticed for two or three months. But when they did, Northpoint's head of benefits at the time canceled the contract immediately. That had been three years ago, and the sales team had finally managed to win the account back—but it had not been easy.

Needing a clearer answer from IT, Jerry grimaces and calls Elrod, who opens with, "Jerry, if you called to apologize, you'll have to get in line. I'm busy at the moment."

"Elrod, you may or may not know that we are having an issue with Northpoint. I need an ETA on the system update," Jerry states plainly. Hearing the sarcasm and sensing the unhelpfulness on the other end, he tries to remain professional. "Can we work together to limit the damage here?"

"Work together?!" Elrod exclaims, raising his voice. "Work toget—" He stops mid-word. "Jerry, I'm going to have to get back to you."

As the line closes when Elrod disconnects, Jerry just shakes his head.

After pausing a moment to collect himself, Jerry rings Cameron to leave a message about Northpoint. Cameron seldom picks up, but on this occasion he does.

"Jerry, I was just thinking about you!"

"Oh great," Jerry replies. "I was hoping to get a quick minute. We have a situation with Northpoint."

"Jerry, we're talking engagement survey action planning and whether to add a floating paid-time-off day or, alternatively, letting everyone work virtually if they want. Which do you think is better? I am trying to wrap this up toot sweet!"

"Umm, well, could we talk about the client issue first? We're in a tough spot there, and the team is working—"

"Those things will work themselves out, as they do," Cameron interrupts Jerry. "Now, virtual or paid time off—what do you think? I'm thinking we go with paid time off. That'll get our scores up. Thanks, Jerry!" Cameron hangs up. Jerry sighs.

How does Cameron get away with being so disconnected? He won't hear a word about IT being unhelpful. As energized as Jerry was walking in earlier this morning to chart a path forward, he feels like a pendulum has swung equally in the opposite direction. He now feels disheartened and frustrated. Why does it need to be this challenging?

He resolves to update his whiteboard with a few key points to focus on tomorrow and synthesize his notes from discussions with Cuthbert. Looking at the whiteboard, Jerry sees that progress is happening on his to-do list, but he can't help but think that the items on the right side are just as important, if in a very different way.

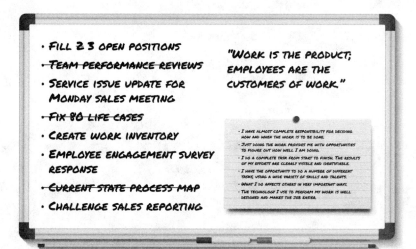

He looks at his watch. He is running late for happy hour.

12

HAPPY HOUR

Remarkable as it may seem, Jerry and three close friends from college—Alicia, Frankie, and Jacob—have been getting together for drinks and conversation once a month since they all graduated from Georgia Tech twelve years ago.

Alicia is a cardiac nurse practitioner, working at Atlanta's highest ranked hospital. She is also very funny, always ready with a quick quip.

Frankie, the most passionate of the clique, works for a nonprofit. She was "mission-driven" even in college, where she got involved in a number of causes, including sustainability, the environment, and social justice. Frankie always seems energized and deeply engaged in her work.

Jacob, his former roommate, is a plant manager for an automotive supplier. Jerry appreciates Jacob's directness and his well-grounded, nuts-and-bolts perspective. Sometimes Jerry misses the obvious—Jacob never does.

After staying later at the office than he had planned, Jerry hurries to the tavern, finding everybody already sitting in their regular booth. He is eager to update them on his latest travails at work, and to get their input.

"Friends, hi, wow, it's been a tremendous couple of weeks," Jerry blurts out.

"What's up, Dr. J?" Alicia asks.

Jerry leads with a question. "Do any of you remember Mike Cuthbert from college?"

"Sure," Frankie says. "Didn't he start a couple of businesses?"

"That's true, and I've been talking with him recently," Jerry shares. "He convinced me that work is broken, to the point that I am aggressively trying to apply some of Mike's research." He explains to his friends the elements of a good, motivating job.

"I am so tracking with you," Alicia says. "That is one of the reasons why I love my job. The work is so important. I am literally saving lives every day. And I have a lot of autonomy in how I do the job, although the doctors can be a real pain in the neck. But I also have some friends in the billing department, which is probably similar to your work, and those people are miserable."

Jerry nods. "So like I said, I am trying to apply this stuff. We are in the thick of this right now with my team at Cons." Jerry adds, "I am learning so much—it's like I'm back in school, only this time it's really helpful in real life!"

Everyone laughs.

Jacob interjects, "That's stuff I see all the time at the plant. We used to have a lot of delivery problems. And the typical, easy answer was always to throw more bodies at it."

"Cuthbert called that the 'easy way.'"

"No, it's not. I can attest to that," Jacob continues. "We finally realized that the people doing the work should really be the ones owning it, so we ended up with reorganizing everybody into smaller teams that are fully empowered."

Jerry interjects, "What do you mean by fully empowered?"

Jacob grins. "They manage their own production schedule. Everybody can stop the line if they find a quality problem. They manage the machine maintenance. It has transformed my life; I can tell you that. You know what we realized? You hire the hands, but you get the brains for free."

"Great line," Jerry remarks. "Okay if I steal that one?"

Jacobs laughs. "Be my guest."

"And so true," Jerry adds. "One of my guys created some automation to eliminate some really tedious, repetitive copy and paste work. I had no idea he could do that."

"We found that as well," Jacob affirms. "We didn't even know what some of their skills were, quite frankly.

"But here's the thing," Jerry reflects. "As encouraging as all of this is, I gotta tell ya that I'm getting, like, little or no support from upper management."

"That's one thing I'm thankful for," Frankie shares. "Everybody in our organization is so focused on the mission. It's a nonprofit of course, so I am sure we are not as rigidly organized as all y'all capitalists, but we try our darn best."

Everyone laughs again.

"Here is something even more disturbing than the lack of support," Jerry shares, knowing he can be authentic with his old friends. "I think a peer of mine is deliberately trying to sabotage me!"

"For real?" asks Alicia.

"Yes, I'm pretty sure," Jerry states. "I don't even know how it got to be this way, but I'm pretty sure that it is."

Jacob sighs and looks at Jerry. "Jerry, I've dealt with my share of workplace rivals. For what it's worth, I'd say you've got to do something, or it'll fester and get worse."

"I'll say!" Jerry blurts. "We had a client issue this week where his IT team was clearly on point to resolve it, and he pretty much just blew me off and did absolutely nothing! And he's apparently upset we took things into our own hands with installing the automation I told you about."

"Jerry, when you start making improvements, you are almost inviting rivals to challenge you," Jacob says. "You're gonna make them look bad for doing nothing. Plus you have invaded his turf and that's a real no-no. Granted, sometimes you have to, but for some people in their own little fiefdoms, that's like a declaration of war. Many people absolutely don't want their status quo disrupted. They resist change, they like things just as they are, and you're threatening them and their little universe."

"I'm not threatening anybody," Jerry retorts.

"Well, of course, you don't mean to," Jacob reassures.

"Don't give in, Jerry," Frankie exhorts. "Don't give in and don't give up."

"That sounds like a fortune cookie," Alicia quips, smiling.

"But seriously, Jerry, what you said about meaningful work is so important," Frankie continues. "And it is a matter of perspective. Have you ever heard the story of the three bricklayers?"

"Oh! I definitely want to hear more about these bricklayers," Alicia says enthusiastically, "as soon as the next round arrives!" Jerry looks over and sees their server approaching the table and bringing a heavy tray weighed down with their refills.

"Okay, here we go," Frankie says, sitting up and looking each of them in the eyes to anchor the story with a little more dramatic energy. "After the Great Fire of 1666 that pretty much leveled London, the world's most famous architect of his day, Christopher Wren, was commissioned to rebuild St. Paul's

Cathedral. A few years later, as the rebuild project was going on, Wren sees three bricklayers on a scaffold. They were each working, diligently laying bricks. One was crouched, one was half-standing, and one standing tall. To the first bricklayer, Wren asks the question 'What are you doing?' to which the bricklayer replies, 'I'm a bricklayer. I'm working hard laying bricks to feed my family.' Wren then asks the second bricklayer, who answers, 'I'm a builder. I'm building a wall.'

"But the third bricklayer," Frankie continues, slowing a bit for effect, "the most productive of the three, when asked the same question by Wren—'What are you doing?'—replies with a gleam in his eye, 'I'm a cathedral builder. I'm building a great cathedral to the Almighty.'"

"Okay, I just got goosebumps," says Alicia.

"I think I've heard that story before," Jacob adds. "So true—it is all about perspective. Now, let's order before the kitchen closes."

Jerry looks at the menu, thinking about getting something to go to bring to Haley. He notices that her favorite dish, the Spicy Cajun Bowl, isn't on the menu. When he asks the server why, she explains that it's been taken off because there was not enough demand.

"Well, that's a shame," Jerry laments.

"The law of supply and demand applies to happy hour as well, my friend," Frankie says with a chuckle.

Her comment reminds Jerry of both the challenge he faces in attracting qualified people and Cuthbert's observation that jobs are a product too.

On his way home Jerry keeps thinking about creating work people truly want to do. That could be a powerful differentiator.

But is it possible? The idea clearly makes sense. But given the cast of characters he has to deal with—Elrod, Cameron, Bellamy— how much room does he actually have to find a better way?

Just as he pulls into the driveway, his phone pings, announcing a new text message. He looks at the screen and then taps to read the message from Cuthbert: "Jerry, sorry, but I need to cancel our meeting next week. I have a board meeting that I need to attend. Let's catch up the week after. Hope all is well. Best, Mike."

He is disappointed; he had been counting on Cuthbert's advice on how to move forward, with the next meeting of the Cow Killers coming up in a few days. He contemplates asking Cuthbert whether they maybe could find another time over the next few days but ultimately decides against it.

Another text flashes on screen. It's Cuthbert again, stating: "Jerry, just to put it out there, you'll be fine on your own. More than fine! Can't wait to hear how it goes."

13

BREAKING THE MOLD

To help inspire and energize the second meeting of the Cow Killers, Jerry has brought doughnuts. And not just any doughnuts but the best doughnuts Atlanta has to offer. He and Haley had discovered the little artisan bakery a couple of months earlier and had become addicted to their extravagant creations and flavors. They were pricey but well worth it. So, armed with $30 worth of doughnut fuel, he enters the conference room where the rest of the Cow Killers are already gathered.

Ryan is the first one to notice. "Wow, Jerry, those things are enormous."

Jerry laughs. "Yes, they are. Your health insurance premium might go up after a couple of those bad boys." Everybody grabs a doughnut and for the next fifteen minutes Jerry basks in the praise of his team.

"I was counting on a bonus, but this will do," proclaims Johnny. "I hereby declare these doughnuts the official nutritional supplement of the Cow Killers."

"I second that motion," Ryan chimes in. "As long as the doughnuts keep coming, you have my undying support."

With food out of the way, Jerry starts the meeting. "Folks, I thought our meeting last week was very productive. We mapped the current process. For today, I would like us to focus on how we could improve the process. Shall we just dive in?"

Mary raises her hand. "Okay, but before we do, I just want to make everyone aware that I'm still pursuing the sales reports issue, but I'm not getting a lot of cooperation. I reached out to Victor from the East region and Shelley from National Accounts to set up a meeting, but they both declined. Then I ran into Marco from Central on the way to the cafeteria, so I brought up the topic and asked him whether we could review the reporting package he gets. He was a bit surprised but was open to a discussion. But we will have to wait until after the big sales meeting Bellamy is organizing next month. I will follow up with him then."

Jerry is a bit disappointed. He had hoped that they would be able to do away with some of the reporting, but there was little he could do about that. "Thanks for the update, Mary. Keep at it. Anybody else have something they want to bring up?"

He waits for a moment and, when nobody speaks up, continues, "For today, I would like us to start thinking about how we could work differently. And to stay true to our name, fellow Cow Killers, there are no sacred cows in this room."

He points toward the process map they put together the previous week. "Any thoughts on this?"

Ryan is the first one to chime in. "Well, I am not sure if this really captures how the work gets done. I mean, this all looks nice and clean, but in reality, there is plenty of back and forth between the teams. There is always something that happens further upstream that creates rework for us. Take the Northpoint case. We had started creating the implementation

Client	Contract signed	Data request						
Broker	Submit contract							
Sales	Log contract							
Prep	Receive contract	Log in system	Estimate workload	Assign to associate	Review client document	Request missing info	Assemble package	Quality check
Setup	Receive package	Assign to associate	Enter data into system	Quality check				
Bill	Assemble package	Create coverage certificate	Create first bill	Quality check				

package for them, but then I learned from Rasheed that we just got another data load, and now we have to do the whole thing all over again."

Johnny nods. "Yes, that's a real problem. I feel we are really working in the dark half the time, with the right hand not knowing what the left hand is doing."

Olivia jumps in. "And there are more handoffs than shown on the chart—since not everybody knows the life system, for example, I am the only one doing those cases. Should we update the chart to show that?"

Jerry thinks about his conversation with Cuthbert and the idea of a whole job. He poses a bold hypothetical: "What if everybody in this group was able to do the whole process? That way there wouldn't be any handoffs?"

Stunned silence for a few seconds.

Mary is the first one to respond. "Jerry, no way. You know how complicated our workflows are; it would take forever to train everybody on everything. And I am not sure everybody would like that."

Johnny adds, "And I don't think that would solve anything.

Our biggest problem is with Sales. They take forever to follow up with the brokers on missing data."

Michele is next. "Well ultimately, it is the clients who create the problems. If they would just give us the correct data from the get-go, we could be much more efficient and much more productive overall."

But Jerry is not ready to give up on his idea. "I hear you guys—" he starts and then catches himself, "—and gals, or better, fellow Cow Killers," which triggers some chuckles, "data quality is a big issue, but we probably make it worse by working in silos. Every time we hand off work, it slows the process down. What if we were to create a team that does a case from start to finish?"

Another pause. Then Johnny speaks up. "That could maybe work. At least it would make sure that everybody is on the same page. It would break down the silos for sure."

Mary counters. "Well, but Michele has a point. Our biggest problem is the quality of the data we get from the client. And neither Sales nor the brokers are particularly energized to help us tackle these issues. They all just care about signing new clients as fast as they can so that they can collect their big fat commission checks."

Jerry has a light-bulb moment. "So, what if we could talk to the clients directly?"

Again, a moment of silence.

"That will never happen," proclaims Johnny. "Sales does not want us to talk to the broker, and the broker does not want us to talk to the client, so that is that."

Michele objects. "Johnny, I am not so sure about that. I mean, you are right that we are not allowed to talk to the clients, or even the broker, as it stands now, but if we could, that would take a lot of the delays out of the process."

"And," Jerry chimes in, "given the issues we have, maybe Sales would be open to revisiting that rule."

Olivia, who has been quiet for a while, jumps back into the discussion. "I like the idea of working in a team."

Jerry had not seen that coming, for he had pegged Olivia as the most change-resistant member of the department. He is not alone in this, and for a moment everyone looks at Olivia with a mixture of surprise and respect for the opinion of the longest-tenured employee in the room.

"If we had a team that is assigned to a specific client case," Olivia went on, "instead of how we do it today, where each part of the process is assigned to somebody else, we would probably be more effective, more coordinated. Everybody could be on the same page."

Ryan quickly follows. "It would actually be cool to see the whole thing from start to finish. Right now, it just feels like I am doing little bits here and there. It just never feels like the job is done. I'm just filling in the blanks all the time."

Jerry nods. "So, it looks like we have two big ideas here. One is to see if we can get Sales to allow us to talk to the clients. That should allow us to address missing data issues faster and more directly right from the source. And the second idea is to have each case assigned to a team that does the work start to finish."

Johnny jumps in. "Okay, I admit those are some big ideas, but what can we actually do?"

Jerry looks at the clock. "Let's take a break before we decide what to do next. Let's take ten."

As the team devours the remaining doughnuts, Jerry thinks

about how far he can go in making changes. Just then Jerry looks out the window and sees the cherry blossoms blooming on the long rows of cherry trees that line both sides of the driveway to the entrance of Consolidated's offices. He thinks about texting Cuthbert. It sure would be nice to get a second opinion right now.

Musing for a moment, seeing the colors and branches, Jerry thinks about the cherry trees that were given by Japan to the United States as a gift. Even though the trees were not native to America, they became transplanted all across the country and flourished seemingly everywhere. How remarkably adaptable. If the cherry trees could adapt, maybe they could too?

They return from break. Jerry looks at the group. "I think we are on to something here. So I would like to see if we can make this work." He looks around the room. "Here is what I would like to propose: Let's try it out. If you are open to the idea, we could form a trial team to pilot a new way of working. Michele, Ryan, and Olivia, I would like you to be the pilot group. What do you think?"

Michele readily accepts with excitement. Olivia agrees, as does Ryan. Jerry looks at Mary and Johnny. "Are you two on board with this? I will need your help to oversee the pilot and assist as necessary."

They both nod, although Jerry notices that Mary seems less enthused. "But what about the other part, getting Sales to agree to us talking to their precious clients?" she challenges.

Jerry grins. "Leave that to me. I think I have an idea for how to tackle that."

"Okay, great," Mary agrees, "but maybe we should wait with all of this until we are fully staffed?"

Jerry feels his level of frustration rising but has to admit Mary has a point. They are already running as fast as they can. Creating the pilot team would certainly take time—precious time they do not have.

But then he has another idea. "I get it; we need more time. So here's the deal. We stop doing the sales reports. Based on the capacity analysis you and Johnny pulled together, that should free up a chunk of time. No more reports for Sales. They can create them for themselves if they want. It's not in our mandate, and it doesn't affect our clients' outcomes."

"Wow, I think our teams will be thrilled to hear this!" Johnny reacts.

"At least until we backfill our open roles. We've got to give the folks in our department a break of some kind," Jerry states firmly.

"Great!" Mary exclaims. "I've never understood why we did those in the first place. But who is going to tell Sales? I am sure we will get some pushback."

"I'll let Sales know in due course," Jerry answers. "I need to talk to Bellamy anyway."

He senses that his decision to stop the sales reports has energized the team. But there are still plenty of challenges.

Johnny points out that there are still a number of things to be worked out. "Jerry, just keep in mind that everybody has open cases they are currently working on, and we need to make sure we don't create new problems."

Jerry admits that he has a point. "You are right, Johnny, we need to plan this out a bit further. And we need to let everybody else know what we are doing," he adds, remembering Cuthbert's advice to involve everyone in the department.

Jerry agrees to use the next departmental meeting to inform everybody about the work of the Cow Killers. He not only wants them to be aware but also wants (and needs) their buy-in and support. He'll clue in Cameron as well.

They conclude the meeting with mapping out the next steps. Jerry will talk to Sales. Mary and Johnny will help set up the pilot team and figure out how to transition the work they are currently doing.

"How quickly do you think we could be up and running?" asks Jerry. Johnny and Mary propose to shoot for the following week. "Four days? I like that ambition. Let's go for it."

The rest of the day goes by quickly. As Jerry is about to leave his office and head home, he sees Eric gingerly approach his office doorway.

"Eric, how are you? What's up?"

"Hi, Jerry. Hey, I just heard we are going to pause all the sales reports?" Eric states, although it comes out more like an uncertain question than a statement.

"Yes, that's right," Jerry replies carefully.

"Well," Eric continues, "that's the best news I've heard in a long time. That is going to help so much. Our client work is so much more important."

Relieved and quite pleased to hear it, Jerry smiles. "Thanks, Eric. I really appreciate hearing that. We are facing some big challenges, being understaffed and overloaded. There is more to come, and we will need everybody here to be willing to step away from the past and step into a better way of working."

"That sounds great, Jerry." Eric looks at him. "Count me in."

Now that was a surprise. Eric had been a mystery to Jerry, although a mystery that he had begun to unravel through Eric's performance review only days earlier. "Thanks, Eric, more coming soon. Thanks again for stopping by." Jerry smiles, trying to convey optimism. That was unexpected but welcome. Jerry recognizes he'll need all the help he can get.

Jerry notices it has gotten dark outside, and the parking lot is largely empty. But for the first time in a long time, Jerry feels excited about a work update to share with Haley when he gets home.

14

FORWARD EVER,
BACKWARD NEVER

Today's the day, Jerry thinks. The first thing he does when he gets to his office is email his team, letting them know that they would discontinue the sales reporting until further notice. Jerry explains that the team is looking at all the options to reduce the case backlog. He summarizes the findings from their inventory analysis and goes on to explain the reasoning behind their decision to stop producing sales reports.

He makes sure to copy Cameron on that note. He contemplates for a second copying the sales leadership team but decides to raise the topic more discreetly when he talks to Bellamy about allowing his group to talk directly to the clients. Which reminds him that he needs to reach out to Bellamy's assistant, Irene, to see when they could meet.

To his surprise, Irene offers him a slot later the same day, at 3:00 p.m. "Jerry, you saved me a phone call," she says. "Bellamy asked me to find some time with you to talk about Northpoint. Will half an hour be enough?"

"We will need more time, Irene. Could we make it an

hour?" He is not surprised that Bellamy wants to talk about Northpoint. He must have heard about the issues they had run into, but now he was a bit worried about the meeting. Would the Northpoint fiasco become a distraction that would impede his reorganization plan?

Johnny slows his pace as he approaches Jerry's office. "Have you heard?" Johnny quietly poses as he pops his head into Jerry's office.

"I don't think so. Heard what?" Jerry replies.

"Elrod apparently emailed a draft memo to Ben," Johnny shares. "A so-called data guru trying to limit and control RPA usage across the company. Apparently, he wants Ben to put everybody on notice that all automation work has to go through him. Looks like he's coming after us, but Tatum got wind of it somehow."

"Yikes. Not helpful. Not helpful at all." Jerry shakes his head.

Though his appetite is diminished, Jerry knows he should head over to grab a bite for lunch before his afternoon meetings. As he passes by Cameron's office on his way back from the cafeteria, turkey sandwich in hand, Cameron waves him in. "You got a second, Jerry?"

"Cameron, how are you?" Jerry asks as he grabs a chair. "What's up?"

"Oh, all fine over here. I saw your note," Cameron shares.

"Okay," Jerry responds, holding, as if more is coming.

"Jerry," Cameron continues, "Did I ever tell you about the time I met a state trooper at the diner?"

"I don't think so."

"Well, this was a good many years back. I was at a diner off the interstate and saw two state troopers having coffee," Cameron begins his story.

Jerry wonders what this has to do with anything.

"Well, they seemed to be finished with their meal and sitting there enjoying their coffee. They seemed to be in pretty good spirits, so I approached them carefully so as not to intrude in case it was unwanted."

"Yeah," Jerry follows along.

"When they eventually noticed me, I asked them if it's not a bother, could I ask them a hypothetical question?" Cameron pauses.

"What was the question?" Jerry asks, mildly intrigued.

"I asked them, 'Suppose you encounter three cars on the interstate speeding, motoring along and they pass you on patrol. You see them speeding, clock them over the limit, and all that.' They look over from their coffee like this happens every, single, solitary day. 'Yes,' they say, 'and . . . ?'"

"Yeah," says Jerry, "not sure I caught the question."

"Right, them neither," Cameron continues. "So, I said, 'You see these cars speeding, passing you. Here's the question—which one of the speeding cars gets the ticket?'"

Jerry is silently cynical. Pointless as he suspects this story is likely to be, now he's curious to hear the troopers' response.

"Jerry, I'm telling you both of the troopers smiled wide and leaned back in their chairs," Cameron goes on. "They look at each other, and the one says, 'Which one gets the ticket? We flash our lights and put on a little chase. The one that gets the ticket . . . is the one that pulls over.'"

Cameron pauses for a moment and looks at Jerry with a twinkle in his eyes, a bit of smirk on his face. "Keep it going, Jerry."

Jerry leaves Cameron's office feeling a bit confused. That had been unexpected. But it seemed Cameron was in support of what they were doing. Maybe he should have used the opportunity to tell Cameron about some of the other changes they were thinking about? But then he remembered one of Haley's favorite expressions: *It is easier to ask for forgiveness than to ask for permission.*

That guidance might well serve Jerry when it came to Elrod as well, but he could barely cease wracking his brain trying to remember where that expression had come from originally. A quick search on his phone revives his memory. That sage advice came from US Navy Rear Admiral Grace Hopper, a brilliant computer programmer, mathematician, and outstanding female pioneer of her day, who had left behind a staggering legacy of innovation.

How could he forget? She was one of Haley's heroes, so Jerry had heard about her often. The full text of Hopper's entreaty was worth saving to his computer:

> That brings me to the most important piece of advice that I can give to all of you: if you've got a good idea, and it's a contribution, I want you to go ahead and *do it*. It is much easier to apologize than it is to get permission.
>
> —**GRACE HOPPER**, "The Future: Hardware, Software, and People"

WIND IN THE SAIL

erry feels a bit queasy as he arrives for his 3:00 p.m. meeting with Bellamy, who has a sprawling corner office on the top floor.

His assistant, Irene, sees him approach. "Right on time, Jerry. Bellamy is still in a meeting with Gordon, but why don't you wait for him in his office? Would you like some coffee?"

Jerry politely declines and settles into one of the enormous leather chairs that line Bellamy's conference table. His office is easily three times the size of Cameron's, Jerry muses.

The door swings open, and Bellamy's bulky frame appears. He had been a promising football star at Georgia Tech before an injury in his senior year ended that career path.

"Just the man I need to see," he exclaims, as he sticks out a big meaty hand. "Good to see you, and thanks for coming up."

Jerry jumps up and shakes hands. "Bellamy, thanks for making time."

They settle into their chairs. Bellamy looks at Jerry. "Let me get straight to the point. I got your message the other day on the case backlog. Now, I understand that you all are overworked and understaffed, but we are being eaten alive by the competition, and our clients are not too happy. And that gets me to Northpoint."

He stops for a second. "Hey, did Irene offer you something to drink? Coffee? Water? Scotch?"

Jerry laughs, a bit forced. "Yes, Bellamy, she did, but I am good."

"Oh, good. Where were we? Ah, yes, Northpoint. Do you know how hard we worked to close that deal?"

Jerry nods, but his silent acknowledgment is apparently not enough for Bellamy.

"I don't think you actually know how hard it was. I mean, we lost that account a few years ago as a result of what these clowns in IT did to mess up the claims system. It took us years to convince them and their broker to give us another chance. And now I hear through the grapevine that their implementation is at risk? Jerry, we cannot let that happen. I don't care what you have to do, but you have to make sure they go live without a glitch." He pauses. "You understand me?"

Jerry squirms in his seat. "Bellamy, I hear you, I really do. And we will do whatever we can to get Northpoint back on track. But to do that, I need your help."

"What do you need from me, Jerry? How can I help?"

"Well, for starters, we need to stop the sales reporting."

"What sales reporting?" Bellamy looks surprised.

"Well, the monthly sales forecast, the commission report, and the broker schemes, for starters," Jerry explains. "They all suck up a lot of time. We have three open positions, and there is no way we can catch up if we need to keep doing the reporting, so," he hesitates for a second before he calmly says, "we will stop producing these reports as of today."

Bellamy looks stunned.

"Well, Jerry, I don't know about that," Bellamy says and pauses for a second. "We need to have reporting. But to be honest, I am not sure I even know what those reports are used for. Monthly sales forecast, you said?"

"Yes, the monthly sales forecast. It provides an estimate of earned revenue by client, rep, broker, region, industry, you name it."

"Jerry, as I said, I am not sure. But I am pretty sure that the numbers I get come directly from Finance. You guys are onboarding."

"Exactly." Jerry senses a window opening. "So, we would like to stop those reports. Well, to be honest, I already told the team this morning that we won't be doing them anymore."

"Oh," Bellamy says, "A *fait accompli*!"

"*Oui, oui*," Jerry replies. "I was hoping that you would back me up. We both know that if we fall behind with onboarding, we will have even angrier clients."

Bellamy nods. "I cannot argue with you there; you are certainly right about that. And since I actually have no idea what those reports are good for, consider me on board with getting rid of them. If anybody on my team complains, we can discuss what they need."

Jerry smiles. "Thank you, I really appreciate your support—which gets me to the second item on my list. One of our biggest issues is the quality of the data we get from clients. A lot of what we need to onboard is missing. We keep sending our requests to Sales, who then reach out to the brokers, who then reach out to the client. In some instances, we cannot proceed without the info we requested. And when we push the cases forward where the data is incomplete, it always bites us later on."

Jerry pauses to see if Bellamy is still tracking with him and then continues, "With bad data in the system, claims are wrong-fully rejected. We already see an increase in customer service calls. So getting the right information as soon as possible from the client into the system is really critical to avoid all that."

Bellamy nods. "Okay, I get that, but what do you want me to do about it? I am pretty sure the account managers and their teams are doing the best they can to get your guys what you need. If the client is not happy, the broker is not happy, and when the broker is not happy, we are not happy."

Jerry leans forward. "Well, I was wondering if we could work directly with the client."

Bellamy looks confused.

Jerry continues, "I have been thinking about this a lot, Bellamy. If my team can talk directly to the client, we can cut out everybody in the middle. I bet that neither the rep nor the broker would mind."

Bellamy purses his lips for a moment and then responds, "That is a very interesting idea, my friend. I like it. Beats me why we have to be in the middle of all this. Quite frankly, most of our account managers are ready to move on before the ink on the signature dries. And you're probably right that the brokers don't want to be in the middle either. But how would that even work?"

Jerry smiles. "I am so glad you ask me that. We have been thinking a bit about how we can change how we work so that we can be more efficient. One of the ideas we have is to create small teams of three people that 'own' a case from start to finish, which is to say, right from when we get the contract from Sales to when we go live and issue the first bill."

Bellamy seems intrigued. "I like that idea. Hey, maybe we can even market it as a premium service. White-glove, concierge-style. But do you think that will work? I mean, do you think your guys can handle the client interaction?"

"Well, we've got good people ready to pilot it. And there is only one way to really find out—to give it a try!" Jerry explains to Bellamy that they already decided to form a small pod with Michele, Ryan, and Olivia.

Bellamy seems to like the idea. "I can see the benefit of that, and I think the clients will like it."

Jerry grins. "Well, I was wondering whether you would be open to use Northpoint as our test case?"

Bellamy is clearly surprised. "Well, that is what I call one hell of a gamble, Jerry. What makes you so sure that this will work?"

"To be honest with you, I don't know. But I know what we are currently doing does not work either."

Bellamy glances at his enormous and very expensive-looking watch. "Jerry, fascinating stuff, but I have another meeting coming up. So, just to summarize what we discussed: You stop the sales reporting for the time being, to be revisited if any of my guys complain. And you want your pods—that is the word you used, right?—to work directly with the clients, meaning the benefits guys. So okay, I agree that we will try this out with Northpoint. If it works, I will discuss this with my guys. I will probably run the idea by some of our brokers as well—you never know. Did I get all that right?"

Jerry nods. "Yes, sir."

Bellamy grins. "Nice sales job, Jerry. Seriously, I cannot believe you talked me into all of this. What do I get out of it?"

Jerry laughs. "Faster and better—and with greater accuracy! Our faster speed and quality will hopefully mean happier clients. And thank you for the nice compliment."

As Bellamy walks him to the office door, he asks Jerry to keep him posted. Jerry is elated. This went a lot better than he thought it would. He decides to reward himself and leave early. Maybe he should take Haley out for dinner?

Having learned from recent experience, he gives her a call. She might have already made other plans. Haley picks up on the third ring and seems excited that he is leaving early. She offers to make a reservation at the same trendy Italian place where they had celebrated their last wedding anniversary. It is not cheap. But Jerry feels he deserves it, so he quickly agrees.

Dinner at Luigi's is again spectacular. Jerry loves Italian food, and Haley clearly enjoys not having to cook for a change. He tells her about his meeting with Bellamy.

"Sounds like a new member of the Jerry Crawford fan club!" she jokes.

Jerry chuckles. "Membership is still in the single digits, honey. Trust me."

"Ah, give it time," she says. "Over time everybody will come to see in you what I see in you."

What a nice compliment. *Two in a single day*, thinks Jerry. Life, at least for the moment, is good.

GOING FAR

For the first time in weeks, Jerry arrives at the office in good spirits, feeling elevated by the support he received from Bellamy the day before.

The Cow Killers will be thrilled, as will hopefully the rest of the department, when he gives an update at today's departmental meeting. Given all that is going on, he extended the meeting, which is typically just half an hour, to a full hour.

Just as he is about to head over to the large conference room, his phone rings. He peeks at the display. Bob, his favorite HR person. He picks up. "Hey Bob, I am about to head into a meeting, so I only have a minute—"

Bob cuts him off. "No worries, Jerry, just wanted to let you know that Meredith accepted the offer. She is ready to start in two weeks. I also checked in with Walter but have not heard back. But hey, one down, two more to go. Oh, and one more thing: My boss approved the supervisor requisition yesterday, so now I just need to get Finance to sign off and then we can post the role."

Jerry is delighted. "Bob, that is music to my ears. You made my day. Sorry, but now I really have to run."

"No worries, Jerry, just wanted to pass on the good news. I will send you the onboarding checklist later today. Talk to you soon."

By the time Jerry enters the room, he is five minutes late. He hates being late but is excited to see some of the team members huddled around the flipchart he had used during the last departmental meeting—and that they are adding their ideas for how they could tackle the backlog. It looks like they have added a few more ideas. Johnny winks at him.

"Hey, boss, we are adding to your list."

"Awesome!" Jerry replies and then apologizes to the team. "Gang, I am so sorry for running late, but I have some exciting news to share."

The team settles into their chairs. "We have a full agenda, so let's jump right into it." Jerry starts off with a recap of their last meeting and reminds the team how critical their work is. He then puts up the capacity analysis. "As you probably heard already, we decided to cut back on reporting, specifically the productivity reports and all of the sales reporting. That should free up quite a bit of time."

Everybody looks surprised, but nobody more than Mary. "But I have not had a chance to talk to Sales yet. Are you sure about that?"

Jerry smiles. "Yes, Mary, I talked to Bellamy, and he agreed to pause the reports. If you hear complaints from anybody in Sales, we will take a look at what they actually need, but for now, no more sales reports." He continues, "And that is not all. I have asked Mary, Johnny, as well as Ryan, Olivia, and Michele, to help me rethink how we do our work. This is a temporary team that will be meeting weekly to figure out a better way. Nothing is off the table, no sacred cows." He pauses a second for dramatic effect. "The team is called the Cow Killers." He sees some grins but also a few startled looks.

Jerry next shows the process map. "We mapped the work-flow and discussed how we can be more effective. And we want to try out a different way of working. Instead of breaking down each case into specific tasks that get assigned to you, we want to create a team that handles each case from start to finish. And Michele, Olivia, and Ryan will test this concept starting next week."

Now Jerry really had their attention. "And there is more," he continues, pointing at the "data missing/changes" bar. "You all know that getting the clients to provide the information we need is a major challenge."

Johnny jumps in. "Well, I would call it a total pain in the butt!"

The room erupts in laughter.

Jerry smiles. "Okay, I talked to Bellamy about that. And I asked him whether we can talk to clients directly, instead of having to go through the account manager and the broker. He will talk to his people but agreed in principle. Oh, and we will get to try this out with Northpoint! Well, the pilot team will."

Jerry points at Ryan, Michele, and Olivia, who by coincidence happen to be sitting next to each other. "So, as you can see, we have been busy trying to find ways to not only become more productive, by focusing more on our core work, but also make your jobs a bit easier." He gazes around the long table. "Any questions so far?"

Rasheed is worried about having to deal directly with clients. Jerry had anticipated this, knowing that as a budding musician, perhaps even someday a songwriter, Rasheed is a very introspective person, not what you would call a conversational-ist. So Jerry explains that the first step is to try out the new way of working with Northpoint, and nothing has been decided yet.

"Rest assured, we will make sure this works smoothly before we fully implement, but I think it will," Jerry says. Then, looking directly at Rasheed, he adds gently, "And we will make sure you are all properly trained."

Hannah is next. "I have been working on the Northpoint disability data, so does that mean I can hand that over to the 'pod'?"

Jerry looks at his three musketeers and wonders, *Are they indeed a structured "pod" or just three guinea pigs at this moment? Full steam ahead*, he resolves. "Yes, but let's have a separate meeting with everyone who has been working on the case. By the way, who else has been working on Northpoint?"

Rasheed, Olivia, Skylar, and Dakota raise their hands, as do Mary and Johnny. *Holy cow*, Jerry thinks, *that's seven people, including Hannah, all working on different pieces of the same account—a recipe for confusion and delay.*

"Okay," Jerry perseveres, "we will set up a meeting to figure this out. Anything else?"

Skylar raises her hand. "Well, Jerry, thank you for the update. But I have a question: Why don't we get doughnuts? Are those only for the A-team?"

Jerry squirms in this seat. This was of course not about doughnuts—Skylar felt left out. And she was probably not the only one. Going into this meeting he had been able to anticipate their concerns about adopting a new way of working; what he had not expected was their willingness, even outright enthusi-asm, to play a role in trying it out. Jerry absolutely did not want to throw cold water on all that refreshing eagerness, and for once, he pivots decisively and plays into it.

"Skylar, you are absolutely right—everybody here deserves doughnuts. And I will make sure we have some for our next staff meeting. And please don't interpret my asking Michele, Ryan, and Olivia to help with rethinking how we do our work as a sign that your ideas are not welcome. They are, and I am very excited to see the ideas you all added to the list we started a few weeks ago. And I will make sure you all will have an opportunity to contribute and add your ideas."

That seems to calm them down. Jerry looks at his watch. Two more minutes. Perfect timing! "Oh, and one more thing." He looks across the room, wondering if any of them picks up on the Steve Jobs reference (Jerry is a huge fan of the late Apple founder), and continues, "In two weeks, Meredith Parker will join our team."

Johnny jumps up. "Great news, boss. I assume that is for the open role on my team?"

Jerry deflects the question. "Well, let's discuss this offline. I just got the news. But for now, that is all the news fit to print. Thanks for your time, everybody!"

The members of Jerry's team start to rise noisily from their chairs, when Michele speaks up loudly. "Uhh, Jerry, everybody?"

Everyone freezes in place. "About that name," Michele continues, "Cow Killers? Do we really want to go with that?"

There is a long silence in the room, until Skylar says, "It does kind of conjure an unpleasant image, doesn't it?" Everyone in the room looks at Jerry as they all sit back down.

Jerry takes a moment to ponder, before decisively issuing his pronouncement.

"Well, it was well intended," he begins, "the idea that every-thing was on the table for scrutiny, no sacred cows. But I have to agree that Cow Killers might be a little hard on the ears of some folks. Perhaps since we are in effect 'going public' with our little experiment across the company, and a lot of other people are going to hear about it, and no doubt are going to be talking about it, maybe we should come up with a more socially con-scious name. Does anybody have any ideas?"

The room goes silent again.

Suddenly, Rasheed laughs out loud, and when everyone looks at him, he declares, "Well, it just sounds to me like we're working on getting our mojo back!"

Now everyone is laughing. "Fine," Jerry says, not wanting to belabor the name. "From now on it's the Mojo Squad, but gang, let's not forget that it's the transformational work that we are trying to accomplish that is really important here, okay?"

He asks Johnny and Mary to stay behind, as everybody else files out of the room. He closes the door. "How do you think that went?"

Mary responds first. "Jerry, I cannot believe you got Bellamy to buy into our plan. Well done!"

"I second that," Johnny adds. "But I also picked up some anxiety from the team."

Jerry nods.

Johnny continues. "Jerry, there is this African proverb that I think applies here. 'If you want to go fast, go alone, but if you want to go far, go together.'"

It takes a second for Jerry to process that. "Well, I definitely want to go far. So, if I understand you correctly, we need to find a way to get the whole department engaged, right?"

Both Mary and Johnny nod.

"Okay," Jerry states, "we will figure out a way to get the rest of the team more involved. But in the meantime, how do you think we are doing?"

Mary replies first. "I think we are doing good. I mean, the backlog is still in the 300s, and it will take a while for the 'pod' to get up and running. I am a bit nervous about starting with Northpoint. Risky move, Jerry."

Jerry looks at Johnny. "What do you think?"

Johnny takes a second to gather his thoughts. "I think we can make this work. But the pod will need a lot of help."

Jerry nods. "It will. And I know you are both very busy, but can I count on the two of you to help us get the pod started? Is that okay?"

They both nod. Johnny volunteers to organize a meeting for handing off the Northpoint work.

17

NEW BEGINNINGS

Haley is booting up the computer in her first-floor office off the family room when Jerry calls out to say goodbye after washing their morning coffee cups and setting them on the drain board. In a way, he envies her working from home. In a way, she envies his daily interpersonal interactions—though not his usually dreaded commute.

"Pilot starts today," Jerry reminds her a bit nervously.

Haley greets him by the door. "And you all will be great. You've been preparing. And remember, be the author of your life. Go write your story forward."

Although he's heard those words so many times before, for some reason they keep resonating today, so much so that the commute somehow seems shorter to Jerry.

He walks into the Cons building and quickly stops by his office, glancing at his whiteboard. As to-dos get crossed off, progress is clearly being made. But much more is needed! Jerry's focus goes to Cuthbert's card.

Seeing it reassures him they're on the right path. Then Jerry heads over to the pilot pod.

Michele, Ryan, and Olivia are engaged in a stand-up meeting

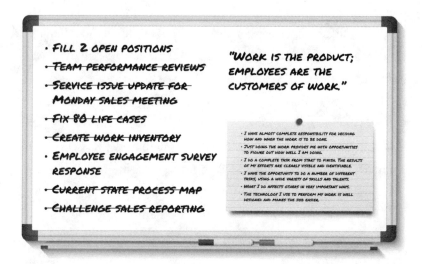

as Jerry arrives. He sees Northpoint work files and the swim lane diagram with key callouts per the teams' deliberations.

The end-to-end workflow now enabled with direct client interactions could be game-changing, Jerry hears the team discussing. *Such enthusiasm is good to hear*, he thinks, believing that his people's eagerness hasn't waned since the earlier departmental meeting introducing the plans.

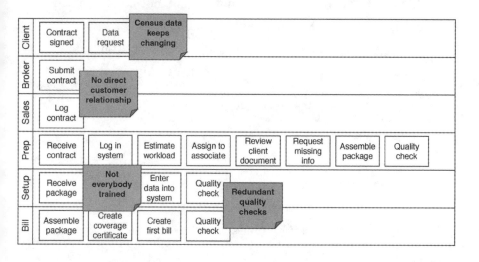

Jerry has just enough time to offer his kudos, encouragement, and appreciation to the pilot team, one and all, when he gets interrupted by a call from Bellamy, who asks if Jerry is available at noon to join him, Shelley (Sales/National Accounts), and Peter (the head of employee benefits at Northpoint).

Fair to update them, Jerry thinks. Though how this gets represented is critical for success. "Would be delighted, Bellamy. See you then."

Jerry returns to the team and asks them to pull together all the information needed from across the entire department—as so many individuals have been connected to Northpoint in one way or another up until now. Better be prepared.

Bellamy has scheduled the meeting over lunch. *Smart move,* Jerry thinks. Breaking bread is always a good relational move.

Jerry can smell the catering as he approaches the client conference room. He and his team are rarely if ever near this side of the complex. *Perhaps that will change in the future,* Jerry amuses himself thinking.

After exchanging pleasantries, Bellamy gets right to it. "Peter, we are here because we know we are not meeting your expectations at present—let alone exceeding them."

"I'm glad you said it before I did," Peter responds a bit tersely. "We decided to give you guys another chance, but we are wondering if perhaps we have made a mistake."

"Please know," Bellamy continues, "we are wholly dedicated to your success. So much so that we are galvanizing a focused effort to fix our issues and give you the results you both want and deserve. Jerry here is going to give you the details."

And with that, Bellamy hands it over to Jerry, who confidently reviews the current status and the various outstanding items before explaining the benefits of the pilot team: direct access to his team, immediate issue resolution, and importantly, less back and forth. Having spent an hour with the pilot team that morning, he is ready to dive into the details.

Peter from Northpoint is pleased and positive. He even agrees to connect Jerry and the pilot team directly to Northpoint's benefits team and to his boss, the vice president of Human Resources.

Jerry sees Bellamy smiling wide as they prepare to adjourn.

Whew. Jerry breathes a sigh of relief heading back to his office. He can't wait to share the news with Haley later.

He sees an email from Elrod as he gets back online. In it, Elrod says he will not approve opening access for Northpoint to a common sandbox for data and document sharing. He has copied his boss Ben, as well as Cameron and Bellamy. Jerry wonders worriedly if he blind-copied Gordon. What is it with Elrod?!

As Jerry is reading it for a second time, he sees Bellamy's reply come through stating that "it is mission critical for that access to be in place ASAP."

Ben quickly aligns with Bellamy by email reply and says he'll support the access. Wow, that was quick. And decisive. Good to have Sales on your side, though Jerry can't help but wonder what Elrod is trying to accomplish by being so adversarial. Meanwhile, Jerry drafts an email to update the team on the day's events. He copies everybody on his team as well, realizing from his staff meeting how important it is to keep everybody up to speed and actively in the loop.

He looks up and sees Johnny passing by. "Johnny, have you got an extra minute?"

"Sure, you bet," Johnny says as he steps into Jerry's office. "What's up?"

"Remember when you asked me about where Meredith would be placed? How about we sit her with the pilot team? To learn the entire process. That could accelerate her training in a big way."

"Interesting idea, and it likely would," Johnny concurs.

"And Meredith has aspirations. She is interested in growth and career development," Jerry continues, "so I want us to structure the work so that it delivers that. A growth experience."

Jerry felt his inner Mike Cuthbert rising. "We are still just getting started."

18

LESSONS LEARNED

B y the time Jerry arrives at his office, Meredith Parker is already waiting for him. She looks a bit nervous, which is not surprising—after all, it is her first day. Jerry gives her an overview about the company and the role of his department. He explains that they are piloting a new approach to onboarding clients and that she will join the pod.

"That is a great way for you to learn the ropes. As part of the pilot team, you will see the whole process from start to finish."

When she asks who she will be reporting to, Jerry hesitates for a second. "Great question. I have asked both Mary and Johnny, who you will meet in a few minutes to oversee the pilot, so for now I would like you to report to both of them."

Meredith looks confused at having two bosses, but nods. Jerry then shows her around the office, introduces her to her coworkers, and takes her to the security office to get her badge. After that, he takes Meredith back to the set of cubicles the pilot team occupies. They have already set up a desk for her.

The pilot team is standing in front of a whiteboard. "Perfect timing, Meredith," exclaims Michele, "you can join us for our daily huddle. This will give you an excellent opportunity to learn about the process."

Jerry lingers for a few minutes, observing the team meeting. The daily huddle is something Johnny had suggested as a way for the team to align on the priorities for the day. So far, these short daily meetings have seemed a very effective way for the pod to keep each other updated and to track progress.

Ryan walks the team through the agenda. "Okay, we are in good shape with Northpoint. Following our first call with the client last week, they have started to provide us the missing census information. And Jeff, their benefits manager, has connected us to their IT department, which should help with testing the data transfer interface. It looks like we will be able to make the go-live date, assuming all goes to plan."

Then they go over some of the open items: Olivia needs training on the new life platform, and Skylar offers to walk her through the system later that day.

"Meredith, why don't you join her for that?" Ryan suggests. "That way we have two people who know how to deal with that platform."

Meredith nods. As their meeting continues, Jerry heads back to his office, passing Johnny in the hallway. "Jerry, do you have a second?"

"Sure thing. Come into my office." They sit down at Jerry's small conference table. "What's up?"

"Couple of things. First of all, it looks like the pod is going well. I have been checking in daily, as has Mary, and it is really surprising how quickly the team has been able to work through the problems. It has been a steep learning curve, but at least from what I hear, they are happy with the new setup."

Jerry nods. "Yes, I had the same impression. I sat in on today's huddle for a few minutes; it looks like Northpoint is getting on track."

Johnny grins. "I have to tell you, the call with the Northpoint team last week went a lot better than I thought it would. Jeff has been very helpful."

Jerry agrees. "Just make sure we keep Shelley in the loop."

Johnny nods. "Already on it, boss. I talked to Shelley, and she told me to call her anytime if I need anything. So far, we are getting great support. But I wanted to talk to you about something else."

He pauses for a second. "I think in a week or so we should be able to take on additional cases. Now, of course, we will still make Northpoint our top priority, but we will have capacity that we should use."

Jerry is excited about the good news. He has been worried about what would happen to their caseload as the pod focused primarily on Northpoint.

Johnny continues, "But here is the rub: If I understood you correctly, Bellamy only agreed to us talking to the customer directly for Northpoint."

"Correct."

"Well, Jerry, I was hoping we could get him to agree to use the same approach for any new cases the pod takes on."

He has a point, Jerry thinks. "So you want the pod to be able to talk to the customer for any of the new cases they take on?"

"Exactly, Jerry."

Now that could create a problem. It was probably a bit too early to go back to Bellamy—they still had to demonstrate that what they were doing actually works.

"Well, I am not sure if we can go back to Bellamy yet. I think we need to first make sure that we deliver Northpoint."

Johnny nods. "Well, I was thinking that maybe we can assign some of Shelley's new cases to the pod. She is already familiar with what we are doing and, as I said, seemed very happy. So if we assign her cases to the team, maybe we can persuade her to introduce us to those customers as well."

Jerry is intrigued but also a bit nervous. "Well, I am okay with that, as long as you stay under the radar."

Johnny offers a mock salute. "Aye, aye, captain. But seriously, I think it will be fine. It has been amazing to see how much more effective we can be when we can talk directly to the customer. I will give Shelley a call and see if she is open to the idea. I will keep you posted."

Jerry nods.

"Great. By the way," Johnny adds, "we need to schedule another meeting of the Mojo Squad. The team wants to take another look at the process. I will be happy to set up the meeting."

Jerry agrees.

After Johnny has left the office, Jerry ponders for a while whether he should let Bellamy know but decides against it. No need to bother him, as long as Shelley is on board.

He is looking forward to tonight's meeting with Cuthbert. It has been a few weeks since they met at the Irish pub, and so much has happened. Jerry is eager to share the progress they have made.

As Jerry walks into the bistro, Cuthbert is already waiting for him. "Jerry, how are you? It has been too long! I cannot wait to hear what you've been up to." The waiter arrives and they order some drinks.

Jerry is eager to bring Cuthbert up to speed. "Mike, I want to start off by thanking you for the great advice you gave me when we last met. We have begun to implement some of the ideas you put in my head. Starting from the inventory of all the work we are doing, sales reporting was a major drag. I talked to the head of Sales, and he agreed that we could pause the reporting for the time being, which has helped a lot."

"Glad to hear," Cuthbert offers.

"And we are starting to make a dent into the enormous caseload we had and are starting to catch up. And even better than that, I got him to agree to let us talk directly to the customer. The team we put together to map the process—we call ourselves . . . well, we originally called ourselves the Cow Killers—you know, eliminating the sacred cows? But after a meeting with the whole department, we decided to tone it down a bit, so now we're the Mojo Squad—as in, working to get the mojo back."

Cuthbert chuckles. "Well, I kinda liked Cow Killers, to be honest, but probably prudent to change it as you did," he concedes.

Jerry smiles and continues, "The team has become a pilot for working differently. We were a bit crazy and decided to give the team the most difficult case we have at the moment. Actually, I think *I* went a bit crazy because that was my harebrained idea. So anyway, in addition to having to figure out how they can best work together, they also need to solve the biggest problem we have. And it seems to be working; we are likely to meet the client deadlines. And since they now actually have some capacity, they will take on new cases, so we will have a chance to see how the workflow could be improved." Jerry pauses. "It has been really rewarding to see the team step up to the plate. They meet every morning to go over priorities, something they came up with by themselves."

Cuthbert smiles. "Jerry, I am so glad to hear that. Being able to talk directly to the customer sounds like a real game changer to me. Should take plenty of time out of the process, all that back and forth between multiple parties. And you created a team that owns the work product from start to finish. Do they sit together?"

"Yes, they do."

"Well, that should improve communication a lot. Also, you seem to be giving them a lot of autonomy."

Jerry ponders that for a moment. "I think you are right. As I am thinking about it, I have given them pretty much carte blanche, and they seem to be perfectly capable of organizing themselves. In fact, we just decided to place our new hire—she just started today—with the pilot team. The consensus is that it will be a great opportunity for her to learn the work top to bottom."

"Wow, nice!" Cuthbert is impressed. "Jerry, here is an idea you might want to consider. You remember the little card I gave you, with those six questions?"

Jerry nods. "Of course, Mike. I have it pinned to my whiteboard and look at it every day."

Cuthbert laughs. "Well, I am honored. So here is the pitch. Take that card and turn it into a survey. Ask everybody in your department to complete it. You can make it anonymous if you want. But either way, make sure you can compare the results from your pilot team with the rest of your team, which I assume is still working the old way."

"Hmm," Jerry says as he listens.

"You might want to wait a bit," Cuthbert adds. "I would give your pilot team at least a month to settle in. I think you will be surprised. Plus, it will give you some ideas as to where you want to go next."

Jerry is intrigued. "That is a great idea. I could do that at our next departmental meeting; it would be a great opportunity to talk about what we are trying to do, and to gauge the initial progress we have made so far." He pauses for a few seconds. "But I have to admit, I am not quite sure what to do next."

Cuthbert leans in. "Well, I think you are well on your way to higher productivity, engaged employees, and satisfied customers. You have started to eliminate non-mission-critical, low-value-added work, which is the first step. It seems that you reinvested some of that saved time to make a dent into your backlog. You created a team that owns the process start to finish, so they are accountable for the entire work product. That is step two. You achieved zero degree of separation from the customer, which is step three. I am very impressed. You are doing great so far."

Jerry smiles and then frowns, "Yes, but what do I do next?"

Cuthbert laughs. "Well, tell me what you think you *should* do. What do you think might be feasible?"

Jerry takes a few seconds to think. "Well, expanding the pilot would be one thing. Assuming that new way of working is better, meaning we are more efficient, we should probably roll that out across the entire department. Now that I think of it, that is a bit daunting. I put the A-team into the pilot group, but I am a bit concerned about how the others will take to it. I am already getting some resistance and also a bit of resentment; some people feel left out. I mean, to give you a stupid example, I brought doughnuts for the team but not for everybody, and they called me out on it. And they are right! So I will have to tread carefully. Plus, it will take a lot of time to get everybody trained up. We have quite a few folks that can only handle really simple cases."

Cuthbert nods. "Granted. But you have time, and you might be able to do things gradually. Plus, you can engage them in sorting out how to get it done. It seems your pilot team is starting to do it."

Jerry nods. "Yes, that is true."

Cuthbert continues, "There is no monopoly on ideas for how to make work better. I am sure the rest of your team has some ideas. Didn't you tell me you had some automation maven in your group?"

Jerry laughs. *Automation maven.* He will have to share that moniker with Tatum. "Yes, I do—although we are making a lot less progress there. Our work is just too complex to do a lot more with it."

Cuthbert nods. "Yes, there are some limits to what the bots can do. But I am sure you will have plenty of opportunities to improve your workflow. As I said before, the direct customer contact should help a lot."

"Well, we hope we get agreement to expand. I mean, we are actually already doing it, but under the radar." He explains to Cuthbert their decision to give all the new National Accounts team cases to the pilot team, given Shelley's support. "We will have to cross our fingers this really works, or I will be really exposed."

Cuthbert raises his hand to summon the waiter. "We will need another round to sort that out," he jokes with an authoritative tone. After they place their order, he looks at Jerry. "I think you are certainly on the right track. It is an experiment, but I think it will work out. Five decades of research into motivation and productivity have shown again and again that employees who experience their work as meaningful, have autonomy to figure out how and when the work gets done, and who know how they are doing outperform those who don't. Of course, it is a major change, but as long as you communicate what is going on, engage everybody in the process, and invest in building their capabilities, I believe you will be fine."

Their drinks arrive.

"Well, we shall see, Mike. I hope you are right. I am still two head count short. And until I fill that supervisor position, we won't be able to do much more."

Cuthbert looks up. "Well, you could ask yourself if you actually need that supervisor role."

Jerry is stunned. "What do you mean by that? Of course, I need to have a supervisor; somebody needs to manage the team."

Cuthbert challenges him. "So those poor employees are currently unmanaged? Probably out of control, breaking all the rules?"

Jerry squirms in his seat. "Well, no, they are doing okay for the time being. But we need the supervisors to assign the tasks, track progress, and of course manage performance, review the work, and provide feedback."

Cuthbert grins. "Well, Jerry, it sounds like your Mojo Squad team is already doing that, no? You said they are sorting out by themselves who does what, and they track their progress with the daily stand-ups."

"Okay, Mike, I give you that, but what about feedback and quality checks?"

Cuthbert laughs. "Well, I would imagine if they all sit together and work on the same case, any issues that arise will be spotted a lot sooner, no?"

Jerry has to admit Cuthbert has a point. "Fine. But what about feedback? Hey, that is one of the key components of motivating work, right?"

Cuthbert laughs again. "I taught you well, young grasshopper. By the way, do you bowl?"

Jerry laughs. "I have not gone bowling in years, but yes. I have knocked over a few pins. What does that have to do with anything?"

"Well, picture bowling blindfolded where you don't see the pins. You roll the ball, you hear some pins fall, and somebody yells 'you knocked down five.' What is the next question you will ask?"

Jerry thinks for a second. "Which five?"

"Exactly." Cuthbert exclaims. "That is the equivalent of the supervisor telling you how you did. As I might have mentioned before, supervisory feedback is only the third-best way to help employees know how well they are performing. The second-best way is feedback from the customer. And I think you will be able to leverage the access to the customer that you now have. Why not let the customers provide the feedback?"

Jerry realizes that Cuthbert is right. Maybe a customer survey is the way to go. "But if that is the second-best way to get feedback, what's the best way?"

"Thanks for reminding me. The best way is that you know just by doing the work how well you are doing. Let's take another sports analogy—golf. You are on the driving range or the course, you can see where the ball is going, and you can make real-time adjustments to your swing." Seeing that Jerry is visibly confused, Cuthbert adds, "I am not sure how easy it is for your team to tell just by doing the work how well they are doing, but you could consider peer reviews, so you have your checks and balances."

While he finds all of this intriguing, Jerry is still uneasy about this "you don't need supervisors" idea, but he has to admit once again that Cuthbert has a point.

Cuthbert, sensing Jerry's hesitation, continues, "Hey, you don't have to make any decisions about this right now. All I am saying is that you might want to think about how you leverage these very experienced leaders you have. I am sure you could leverage their skills and experience in better ways than assigning tasks, completing reports, and checking for errors. Maybe they could do more training and coaching?"

Cuthbert glances at his watch. "Jerry, this has been a lot of fun. As I said before, you are doing great, and your heart seems to be in the right place. I'm convinced this will work out even better than you think it could. I cannot wait to see what you do next. Let's connect in a month or two; I will be traveling a bit. We are raising some money for our new venture."

Jerry feels bad, realizing that he has monopolized the situation. He did not even ask what was going on in Cuthbert's world. "Mike, I know we are out of time, but I would love to hear more about your new business venture, maybe next time?"

Cuthbert grins. "No worries, and sure, I'll tell you more next time. But in the meantime, keep up the good work!"

As Jerry pulls onto the highway, he realizes that they never finished the conversation about what comes next. Well, actually not true—Cuthbert gave him a couple of ideas. The rest, Jerry realizes, really has to come from him.

As he walks into the house, Haley is sitting in the family room reading. She glances at him. "Greetings, stranger. How was your meeting with your friend Mike?"

"It was great, honey. He was very complimentary about some

of the changes I have been making at work. And I always walk away with a lot of ideas and some great advice, which I should probably write down before I forget them."

She waves him away, laughing. "You go, Jerry, and write down your unifying theory of management. I will be holding down this sofa and finishing my spy novel."

He retreats to his home office and starts to capture on paper some of the insights he gleaned from Cuthbert. He jots down the three transformational steps (eliminate non-mission-critical, low-value-added work, create ownership for the entire work product, create direct customer relationships), the three elements of driving change (communicate, engage, educate), and finally, the three ways of getting feedback.*

He also creates an action item to survey the department on work design at the next staff meeting. By the time he is done, it is almost 11:00 p.m. Haley is already asleep, snoring up a storm. Jerry sneaks under the covers and falls asleep despite the noise coming from the other side of the bed. It has been a long day and Jerry is spent.

---

* A concise summary of Jerry's notes is included in the appendix.

GO BIG OR GO HOME

It has been nearly three weeks since his last meeting with Cuthbert. Today is his departmental meeting, and Jerry is eager to share what they have learned so far from the pilot and get the whole team more engaged in the journey. And they have learned a lot since unleashing the Mojo Squad. Not only has the team been able to get Northpoint back on track for going live, but they have also taken on all of Shelley's new cases. And those are on track too—which is easy for everybody to see, since the team actively tracks progress using part of the large whiteboard they had Johnny install for them on the wall behind their huddle of desks.

The board shows the progress of each case against the deadline and the top issues everybody is working on. Jerry also notices that they have started to train each other on their respective areas of expertise, which has helped a lot with moving cases along when somebody is out.

But he is most impressed with how quickly Meredith has come up to speed. She has gone from knowing nothing about onboarding or insurance to now being able to handle seamlessly some of the more complicated cases from start to finish.

And he is starting to see some anecdotal evidence that they are making real progress in reducing the time it takes to process a whole case. The first of the new cases from Shelley was completed in less than two weeks. Yes, it had been a simple case, but the sheer fact they were able to get the case implemented so quickly had prompted a call from Shelley congratulating him. She even promised to let Bellamy know how happy she was with the Mojo Squad.

So, there was plenty to talk about at this meeting. Plus, he had promised Cuthbert that he would survey the team on how they experienced their work. Tatum had helped him set up the survey using a simple web interface, which would allow everybody to answer the questions anonymously and summarize the results in real time.

Jerry starts off the meeting with an apology. "Everybody, I know the last couple of months have been very stressful, and I appreciate the hard work every single one of you is doing. And I apologize for Doughnut-Gate last month," Jerry pauses for a few smiles and laughs, "so first of all, I would like you all to dig into those bad boys," as he points to a table near the back with four boxes of Atlanta's finest doughnuts, enough to feed a small army.

After everybody loads up their plates (Skylar manages to fit three on hers), Jerry continues.

"I think we are starting to turn the corner," Jerry states confidently. "Pausing those sales reports seems to have helped a lot." He looks around the table and sees some nods. "We are starting to reduce the backlog of cases somewhat. I think our backlog is below 300, is that right, Mary?"

Mary nods affirmatively.

Jerry continues, "And, as you know, we started a pilot team consisting of Michele, Ryan, Olivia, and Meredith, which has been focusing on Northpoint initially, as well as the new cases coming from National Accounts." He pauses for a second but decides not to share how delighted Shelley is. "So now we have two ways of working, and while it still remains to be seen whether the new way is working better, I would like to do a little survey of how each of you experiences the work you are doing. It is a short survey, seven questions; it is anonymous; and Tatum set us up with some cool tech." He flashes up the QR code on the screen. "Please scan the code; it will take you to the survey. Let's all take ten minutes to do this, and then we can review the results."

Jerry grabs a doughnut for himself while he watches everybody scanning the code and completing the survey on their phones, while they are devouring the doughnuts. When everybody is done, he looks at Tatum. "So, what's the verdict?"

Tatum grins and plugs his laptop into the projector.

Jerry had not expected to see such a dramatic difference between the scores of the pilot team (black) versus everybody else in the conventional teams (gray)—especially after such a short time. Could that be right?

Looking around the table, Jerry realizes he is getting a lot of confused looks. "Sorry, I should have done a better job explaining this. As I said, the purpose of these questions is to understand how you experience your job. And from what it looks like, the black team, which is the pilot group, seems to have a better experience, presumably as a result of the experimental changes we have implemented. I would like to use this meeting to get everybody up to speed on what we are doing differently over there, as well as get your ideas on what else we can improve."

Category	Question	Fully disagree	Disagree	Somewhat disagree	Neutral	Somewhat agree	Agree	Strongly agree
Autonomy	I have almost complete responsibility for deciding how and when the work is to be done.		▓	▓		█		
Feedback	Just doing the work provides me with opportunities to figure out how well I am doing.		▓	▓	█	█		
Entirety	I do a complete task from start to finish. The results of my efforts are clearly visible and identifiable.	▓				█	█	
Variety	I have the opportunity to do a number of different tasks, using a wide variety of skills and talents.		▓	▓		█	█	
Purpose	What I do affects others in very important ways.			▓	▓	█	█	█
Technology	The technology I use to perform my work is well designed and makes the job easier.	▓ / █	▓	▓				

Jerry is surprised when Eric is the first one to say something, with deadpan delivery. "But we all agree that the technology around here sucks." For a second everyone is stunned, and then the room erupts in laughter. And happily, it seems as though that laughter relieves the tension.

As the laughter subsides, Skylar speaks up, looking at the Mojo Squad section. "I am curious as to why y'all think this job is great all of a sudden?" There is a bit of an edge in her voice. The Mojo Squad look at each other.

Ryan is the first to respond. "Well, it was a bit overwhelming at first when Jerry threw us to the wolves, I mean, by asking us to take on Northpoint. It was a mess at first, but as we started digging in, we saw that by tackling the case as a team and by being able to talk directly to the client, we could be so much more effective."

Michele jumps in. "We get answers to our questions much faster now. And once we started taking on new cases for National Accounts, we really saw the benefits of doing each whole case together. Everybody knows what is going on—the current status, as well as what still needs to be done."

Olivia closes the loop. "I have been here for a while and I thought I really knew the process, but by sitting side by side and working together, I have to admit even I have learned a lot."

Rasheed, who rarely says anything, is next. "So, who does the scheduling?"

Ryan laughs. "We all do. We have a quick daily stand-up where we talk about what needs to get done. And we figured out how we can use the whiteboard to track our cases."

Eric looks at Jerry. "So, when can the rest of us try out this worker paradise?" Jerry notices a hint of sarcasm but also real curiosity in his voice.

"Excellent question, Eric. It looks to me like this could be a much more effective way of working, but it is a bit too early to tell. That said, the early results are quite promising. And I want you all to be part of this. I am sure you all have ideas that can help us take this even further."

Hannah pipes up. "Jerry, that sounds like you want us to take on a lot more responsibility. Does that mean our pay goes up?"

That question catches Jerry off guard, and everybody in the room notices it. "Well, Hannah, that is a really good question. I have no immediate answer for you. But if we really become more productive and make clients happy, I think that is something we can discuss." Jerry knew that he was treading into uncharted waters. HR owned the salary ranges, and he suspected increasing their salaries across the board might be a really tough battle. But he also knew that if he really wanted his team to take on more responsibility, they should expect more pay. He purposefully scans the faces of the entire team as he says in a serious tone, "I don't want to make any promises I cannot keep, but if we can really pull this off, I promise you I will go to bat for you on this."

That seems to satisfy the group. Tatum asks about next steps. "Thanks for bringing that up, Tatum. I would love to replicate what we are doing with the Mojo Squad," Jerry nods to the team huddled in the corner, "as soon as we can." He looks around the room. "Anybody here interested in helping us figure out how to make that happen?"

Eric raises his hand. "I would be interested in working on this, but obviously I can't do it by myself."

And then, to everybody's surprise, Dakota, who also almost never says anything, raises her hand, looks at Jerry, and volunteers, "I'll work with Eric."

Jerry is blown away. Eric and Dakota, what a pair! But he is excited that there is some solid engagement. "Terrific!" he exclaims. "We will really need to think this through—the training needed, the timeline, and of course we will still need to convince Sales to allow all of us to talk to customers directly, but we can definitely start planning." Jerry looks at his watch. "We've got a few minutes left, so maybe we start wrapping this meeting up." He summarizes the next steps. "Team, I think we are just at the beginning of an interesting journey—and I am really excited, and just to reiterate what I said earlier, I want all of us to be part of it. More to come, more to come."

20

BULLETS FLYING

May 1. The go-live date for Northpoint has finally arrived. Jerry makes a point to show up extra early—just in case they run into any problems. He is delighted to see the Mojo Squad already at their desks; they clearly know how important this day is going to be.

"Howdy, Mojo Squad. How are we doing?"

Ryan looks up. "We are good to go, boss. We had the final test run with the Northpoint folks last night, and as of now all of their employees should have their cards and policy manuals and be able to access the portal. We also checked that we have the latest census and that the data feeds work. Tatum was able to build us a little bot to automate logging in to all these provider portals, and that is a life saver."

First time I'm hearing about that, thinks Jerry. But he delights in seeing Tatum taking the initiative and applying his unique skills. *What if everybody would work like that?* he wonders.

"Excellent. Well, I hope it all goes off without a hitch. When will we know?"

"We should know soon. Johnny reached out to the Customer Service folks to let us know if they get any calls from Northpoint."

Jerry smiles. *Good move, Johnny. Customer Service would be the first to know if something went wrong.*

"Sounds like you got it all covered. Well, I am in my office if you need me."

As Jerry enters his office, the phone rings. He checks the caller ID. *Ben, the CIO? What does he want?* Jerry picks up the phone. "Hello, Ben—what can I do you for?"

Ben had joined Cons at about the same time as Jerry, but they had not had much interaction. Jerry had participated in a couple of meetings with Ben, most of them related to system projects. He was mild-mannered, bald, and wore thick glasses but was very personable and friendly. And he had a strong southern drawl, from Alabama if Jerry remembered correctly.

"Well, Jerry, we have a problem. I understand you have installed some unauthorized software on our system?"

Jerry is stunned. He mumbles, "You mean the RPA software we are using?"

"Precisely."

"Who told you that?"

"Elrod brought it up."

Jerry's blood pressure rises. *What the hell was wrong with that guy? His mind is racing.*

"This is not an April Fool's joke, is it?" Ben asks bluntly.

"No, I can assure you it is not." Pause. Then Ben presses on. "Well, Jerry?"

Offense is the best defense, Jerry thinks. *Let's not get pulled over here.* "You are correct," he replies assertively. "We are utilizing an

RPA package to automate some of the manual work we have to do here, given the lack of integrations."

The moment he says those last words he regrets it. "Sorry for the dig," he adds quickly, "we love our friends in IT, but we also were told that we should not expect any help, given the big claims system project. And I happen to have somebody in my group that knows a bit about RPA. And it helped us a ton when we had to tackle the issue with the life product. But if we broke anything—"

Before he can even finish his preemptive apology, Ben interrupts.

"Jerry, please forgive my ignorance. This is all news to me. Do you mind if we unwind this thread a bit?"

"Sure, Ben. You recall we launched the life product at the start of the year?"

"Yes, of course. Everybody keeps raving about that."

"Well, that is great, but somehow the dataflow between the life system and the policy admin system does not work," Jerry explains. "We had a huge backlog of cases on our hands that we would have had to manually enter into the system—meanwhile the Customer Service team would be inundated with calls from employees trying to enroll in the life product."

Ben sighs. "So, when that happened you were told that we cannot help you?"

"No, Ben, not exactly. I was told back in January that I better take a number when it comes to any system issues, since Claims rules supreme."

The silence on the other end speaks for itself.

"Jerry, I apologize. It sounds like we let you down. Yes, the new claims project is important, but we should be able to help you guys, regardless."

"Thanks, Ben. And I agree. I mean, the data feed was part of the requirements, and I am a bit surprised that nobody bothered to check that it works. And since it clearly does not, that should have been put in the queue automatically."

"You are right, Jerry. But I also think Elrod has a good point. How do we know we are not creating a big security issue here? I think the best path forward is to shut this down for the time being, until the IT security folks can do an audit. Would you be okay with that?"

Jerry has to think about that for a moment. It would probably be a bad idea to piss off Ben. On the other hand, switching off the robots would bring back all that manual work. Jerry decides to push his luck.

"Ben, I have a counterproposal," Jerry says. "We are in the midst of going live with a large new client, Northpoint. We lost them a couple years ago, but Bellamy won them back. I have a team focused on making sure they go live without a hitch. The bots are a critical tool for the team; if we shut them down now, we will drown in manual work. Remember, that interface is still not fixed. So, unless you are willing to give us a few folks to manually key in data and check systems, I propose we keep the bots running. And if your security folks want to look at it, we can schedule some time." Jerry pauses, for dramatic effect. "But if you disagree, I suggest you talk to Bellamy, since it is his client." Drop mic.

Jerry feels bad for a second putting the screws to Ben, but to his surprise Ben is not upset. "Jerry, I agree, that's a very reasonable suggestion. I'll ask our security folks to reach out to you to schedule a meeting. Hey, maybe we can use those tools in other parts too? If one of your guys can get it to work, it can't be that difficult. I mean, of course I have heard about RPA, but to be honest, I have never seen it in action."

Jerry laughs. "Ben, why don't you come down when you have time and talk to my team member Tatum, who is the genius here."

"Jerry, I will take you up on that," Ben says, sounding intrigued. "Everybody keeps talking about this, and I get it intellectually, but it would be great to see how involved it is."

"Well, I have just the guy you should talk to. Whenever you want."

There is a pause.

"Hey, Jerry, this was very insightful. Thank you for the conversation. But, before we hang up, there is one other thing I think you should know." He pauses. "You will hear it anyway, or maybe already heard? We are looking at a shared services concept. We think that if we consolidate all the transactional work we could get some great economies of scale and also could find some lower cost resources."

Jerry cannot believe what he is hearing. "Sorry, Ben, this is the first time I'm hearing about this. So, if I understand you correctly, there is a project to create a shared services group, which would include what?"

"Customer Service, of course; Claims; your team . . . basically all the transactional areas. Elrod thinks there are some real cost savings if we pool all that kind of work into one team and manage it like a factory."

Jerry is speechless. It takes him a few seconds to respond. "Well, Ben, thanks for the heads-up, but I think that's a terrible idea. So what stage are these discussions in?"

"Elrod just pitched it to Gordon yesterday, and he agreed to move forward with building a detailed business case and project proposal." He pauses. "I am sure you will be able to provide some input." After another short pause he continues. "Hey, good luck on that Northpoint launch. Bellamy told me how hard he had to work to win that business back, given how badly it went the last time."

Jerry laughs. "Thanks, Ben. And thanks for the conversation—and for the heads-up."

He hangs up. Wow. Yes, he and Elrod had not been friendly for a while, but this was a bold move. Of course, the creation of a shared services department would run directly counter to the direction Jerry was presently headed. Thinking about his conversations with Cuthbert about what makes a good job, Jerry realizes that the proposed model would create the exact opposite: every task broken into discrete bits and pieces, governed by a ticketing system. That, in turn, would pretty much be the complete opposite of owning the work product and being able to use a variety of skills. And it certainly wouldn't engender any feeling among his team that the work they do is important, or that it matters that much to Consolidated's clients and their employee plan subscribers. Autonomy? Forget about it. And being able to tell how you are doing by doing the work itself? No way.

Jerry cannot let that happen. Not now, just as they are starting to see some real, promising signals. But the first priority is to get through the Northpoint launch. He is startled by an abrupt knock on his door. It's Bellamy, looking stern. "Got a minute, big guy?"

"Sure, Bellamy, what's up?"

"Well, I just wanted to let you know that I got a call from Northpoint's head of HR this morning." He drops the poker face and starts to grin. "Jerry, I don't know how you guys did this, but the Northpoint team is very happy. He even offered to be a reference for us. Incredible." He pauses. "Please take everybody on the team out for a nice meal, on my dime. I mean it."

Jerry is relieved. "Bellamy, that is great news. I will pass this on to the team. They did all the hard work. By the way, you played a big role in this. Without us being able to talk directly to the clients, we would not have been able to pull this off. I know you took a risk with that."

Bellamy grins. "Well, about that, Jerry," he starts, pausing for dramatic effect, "I understand all of Shelley's cases are now getting the same premium treatment?"

He is not surprised Bellamy already knows. "Well, the team we dedicated to Northpoint had some free capacity, so they started working on some of her team's new cases, and it just seemed easier to use the same approach."

"Well, you made her really happy. She told me that you guys are now able to implement a new case in two weeks!"

"Bellamy, that was a bit of an outlier, an easy case, plus the team using the new process does not have to deal with the backlog of current cases. But we are looking into rolling out those changes across the board. Once we know it really works, of course."

"Well, all I can say is that I cannot remember a client calling me and telling me that they are happy with their onboarding experience," Bellamy shares. "Hey, half the time I have the head of HR yelling at me because we messed up some senior cat's visit to the ophthalmologist. So, whatever you are doing seems to work. Keep it up. And let me know if there is anything I can do to help."

Jerry knows when to seize an opportunity. "Well, Bellamy, actually there are a few things I could use your support on." He pauses and then continues. "First, if we decide to go live with the new process across the board, we will need to be able to talk to the clients—so that will require some communication and senior management push to make that happen. I am not sure if the brokers will be as supportive as you and Shelley have been, and the other sales folks will probably require a little positive reinforcement about the idea."

Bellamy nods. "Well, you have Shelley and me in your corner, and I doubt that any of my sales guys really enjoy sitting in the middle. As long as you keep the sales lead and the brokers in the loop so they know what is going on, they should be okay. And if not, I will remind everybody that their fat commission checks will only continue if the clients are happy—as happy as Northpoint."

"That is music to my ears," Jerry says. "I will let you know when we are ready to flip the switch."

"You can count on me—and on Shelley. She even asked whether you guys should move over into the Sales organization, given how important the whole customer experience is. She would love to have her own onboarding team."

Now that was not exactly how Jerry had anticipated the conversation to go. His team becoming part of Sales?

"Bellamy, we appreciate the support. On that last point, I am not so sure. Of course, the idea is intriguing, but I think the priority for now is to roll out the new process across the rest of the team, which will require a lot of training and change management." He pauses for a second. "But the idea of aligning ourselves with the Sales organization is an interesting one. Let me get back to you on that. Maybe we can make Shelley happy without moving offices."

Jerry takes another pause. "And just to be transparent, I just heard this morning there is some initiative that might jeopardize some of the things we are trying to do for you, for the brokers, and for the clients." He can see he has Bellamy's attention now. He shares with Bellamy what Ben had told him about the shared services project. "Obviously, that would kind of dismantle what we have been trying to do—and what seems to work. I don't think Elrod's plan includes teams owning the entire onboarding process, talking to clients, managing their own work, and so on. I assume his model will look more like the Customer Service function." Jerry could see he had hit a nerve.

"Absolutely no way!" Bellamy blurts out. "Customer Service is a complete disaster, and it's killing us when it comes to renewals. Nobody over there really knows the business. Last time I heard, turnover is 50 percent, so the average hire lasts only two years. I mean, I saw the engagement survey scores, these guys are rock bottom."

Jerry nods. "I couldn't agree more. It would be a disaster. I heard about it today for the first time, so maybe there is still time to stop this. Well, you are part of the senior team, so you are probably the first to know."

"Jerry, I will definitely keep my eyes and ears open."

"Great. Oh, there is one more thing."

Bellamy laughs. "Okay, enough with the Steve Jobs imitation."

Jerry grins, and then proceeds to explain the RPA issue, and why the robots were so important. "You might get a call from Ben, who seemed eager to shut us down. I think I was able to dissuade him, but you might hear from him directly. I would appreciate your support."

Bellamy chuckles. "No problem, Jerry. I think Ben is smart enough to not get into a pissing contest with Sales. You let me know if you run into any problems."

After Bellamy leaves, Jerry's thoughts return to the shared services project. He wonders if he should reach out to Elrod but decides to wait. Ben had said there would be opportunities to provide input. But he should probably be prepared. Thinking of it, he should probably start collecting some hard data to support his position. Maybe Johnny and Mary could help him with that. Jerry checks their calendars and grabs an open slot for the following day.

Time for lunch. Jerry heads down to the cafeteria but cannot resist swinging by the Mojo Squad to get a status update. As he approaches the cluster of tables, he is surprised to see nobody at their desk. Jerry then realizes that the entire team is sitting in the small conference room across the corridor, huddled around a speakerphone. He heads over, and as he approaches, Johnny waves him in. Jerry grabs an empty chair.

Johnny whispers, "We are talking to Northpoint. They have an issue." In an instant Jerry's face goes pale. Johnny quickly shakes his head and adds, "It's their issue. Not ours." Relieved, Jerry sits back and starts to follow the conversation. He recognizes the voice of Peter, Northpoint's benefits manager, whom he had met only a few weeks earlier.

"Guys, you have been an incredible partner these last few weeks, and I know we just went live, but if you could help me out with this."

Michele responds helpfully. "Peter, no worries. We will take care of it. We should be able to get it done by the end of the week, so I hope that works on your end?"

Jerry wonders what this is all about, but Peter is apparently delighted. "That would be fantastic. Thank you!"

After the call ends, Michele explains. "Their benefits department completely forgot to send us the data for a small off-site team. Apparently, those folks had no access to the sign-up portal, so they filled out paper forms, which somehow got lost in some kind of internal shuffle. Peter was asking whether we could get those employees set up."

"And you told him we could do that by the end of the week?"

"Yes, Jerry. There are a couple of things we can do in parallel, so this is no big deal."

"That is amazing." Jerry smiles. "Well, to add on to that, Bellamy just asked me to take you all out for a nice meal."

The team cheers, but Johnny has a question. "Jerry, that is very nice of Bellamy, but don't you think we need to include the entire department? I mean, without all of them covering for us while we figure out a better way of working, we wouldn't be there."

Jerry suddenly relives the horror of Doughnut-Gate—how on earth could he have forgotten? "You are absolutely right," he declares. "We'll all go out for a nice meal. I'm sure Bellamy won't mind."

Jerry suddenly remembers why he came into the room. "So, how are things with Northpoint overall?"

"It went off without a hitch, Jerry, just as you hoped," Johnny offers, and the others nod.

"Well, that is awesome. Please keep me posted."

Some twenty minutes later, Jerry is standing in line at the cafeteria cash register, waiting to pay for his lunch. He hears a familiar voice behind him and notices Elrod with two other men in suits a few feet behind. The two suits are wearing visitor badges. Vendors?

It his turn to pay, and by the time Jerry grabs his tray and finds a spot at an empty table to eat his sandwich, he has already forgotten the brief encounter.

Sitting in rush-hour traffic, Jerry realizes that for the first time in weeks he feels a sense of tranquility and quiet satisfaction. They really pulled it off! Northpoint went live without a hitch—in actuality, it went off *despite a hitch* created by Northpoint that *his team fixed* without a hitch! Bellamy and Shelley are happy. What had Cuthbert told him? It seems like eons ago. Thinking back, Jerry recalls: *improved productivity, satisfied customers, engaged employees.* Yes, it was possible to achieve all three.

Now it was time to expand the pilot to the entire department. He makes a mental note to check in with Eric and Dakota. They probably have not even started on the training plan yet.

When he walks into the house, he sees a card on the kitchen table. "Having dinner with Daphne. Love, Haley. P.S. There is leftover pasta in the fridge."

Bummer. Jerry had been looking forward to celebrating the Northpoint success a bit. He glances at the leftovers. Not really enticing. But beggars can't be choosers. He opens a bottle of wine and scarfs down his food and then retreats to the family room to watch TV. When Haley walks in the door close to eleven, Jerry has fallen asleep on the couch. She gently wakes him up, and half asleep he follows her to bed. "Had a good day, hon?" she asks.

Jerry yawns. "Best day in a while. Can't wait to tell you more about it, but right now I need to sleep."

She laughs, but Jerry was not joking. The moment his head hits the pillow he is down for the count.

21

ALL IN

Mary and Johnny are already in the conference room, chatting over coffee, when Jerry opens the door and greets them with a cheery, "How is everybody?"

After exchanging some pleasantries, they sit down. "So, what are we talking about? How to turn everybody into a Mojo Squad member?" jokes Johnny.

Jerry cannot suppress a grin. "Well, we should, and we will. But there is something I need to tell you first." He pauses. "Have you heard about the shared services project?"

Both Mary and Johnny shake their heads. "No, Jerry, we have not. What is it all about?" Mary replies.

"Well, first of all, it is still on the drawing board as far as I know. So there is no reason to freak out." From the looks on their faces, he could tell that he was clearly succeeding if he wanted to freak them out.

Jerry quickly continues: "Apparently Elrod is working on some proposal to combine all the transactional teams—meaning Customer Service, us, and probably some parts of Claims, HR, Finance, and Procurement—into a large central team. All based on the idea that if we put all these groups together, we could get economies of scale—*and* find cheaper labor."

Now they are really freaking out. "Who told you that?" asks Johnny nervously.

When Jerry explains he heard it from Ben, Johnny shrugs, saying, "Great. Another scintillating idea delivered to you by IT. Did they already forget about the life project?"

Jerry nods.

Then Mary chimes in. "But you said this is still in discussion, right?"

"Yes." Jerry pauses, thinking about the two suits he had seen with Elrod in the cafeteria. He had not made the connection then—or perhaps subconsciously he has simply avoided doing so—but those guys were probably consultants working with Elrod. And if that was the case, then the project was probably a lot further along than Ben had suggested. Jerry considers for a second not sharing that piece of information, but better that they should know everything. "And I saw Elrod in the cafeteria with some suits. I didn't think about it earlier, but now I'm wondering whether they were maybe consultants working with Elrod on this. Those suits looked expensive, and they didn't look like your typical software vendors, unless I'm crazy."

Johnny's and Mary's faces show a mix of anxiety and frustration. Johnny is the first to break the silence. "Well, I have heard about shared services. My brother ran an HR operations team for a few years. The idea on paper makes a lot of sense, but from what Jimmy told me, the reality is not so rosy."

Mary nods in agreement, adding, "Seems to me this goes against everything we have been trying to achieve with the pilot."

Jerry grimaces. "That's my concern as well. I suspect that the basic idea is to break everything into small pieces, so they can find cheaper resources to do the job while—"

"And then ship the work off to India or the Philippines!" Johnny interjects.

"Yes, I would not put it past them, Johnny, but honestly, I do not know. All I know is that they are talking about it. Ben seemed to think that it was still in an early stage."

The room falls silent for a second. Then Mary speaks up. "So we still have a chance to make our case."

Jerry nods. "Exactly. That is why I called this meeting. I think we need to start considering how we tell our story."

They brainstorm for a few minutes about how to do that. "We need to show that the Mojo Squad model is much more effective than the old approach," Mary argues, "so we better start collecting some data."

Johnny agrees. "And some customer feedback. Well, customer, broker, Sales—everybody and everything helps. We need some strong advocates."

"Well, Sales is on our side," exclaims Jerry. "Bellamy and Shelley have bought in, pretty strongly, I might add. Shelley even asked to have her own onboarding team."

Johnny laughs. "Hilarious! Can you believe it?! Until three months ago everybody was yelling at us, and now they want to take us over? What did you say?"

Jerry smiles. "I told Bellamy that I take that as a compliment, but it's probably not something we would want to do. Plus, I don't think it would be very effective."

Johnny nods. "Agreed. But maybe we can meet them halfway. We could have a bunch of pods, each aligned to a specific sales team, so the salespeople get what they want. And we still retain the flexibility we need."

Jerry has to admit that is a pretty good idea. "Johnny, I like it. Let's make that part of our plan for rolling out the Mojo Squad concept."

Mary interjects. "Well, maybe we should wait with that. I mean, wouldn't we be better off sticking with the old concept for the time being? I agree that the Mojo Squad concept is the way to go in the long run, but shouldn't we put some points on the board by getting through the backlog first? Switching everybody over to the new model will be a major change and we will take a hit on productivity. Our backlog could increase instead, at least initially."

The room falls silent. Mary had raised a powerful argument. Then Jerry speaks up. "I will paraphrase some Tom Petty here: 'We won't back down.' We all know that the Mojo Squad way is the right way. You both have front-row seats. The pilot team is much more engaged. True or false?"

"True," Johnny replies.

"Are they able to complete cases faster?"

Johnny nods, but Mary shakes her head. "Jerry, I don't think we know that yet. Yes, they did a case in less than two weeks, but that was one of their first cases, so there was no juggling involved. And with respect to Northpoint, that was Bellamy's client—his 'baby'—so we threw all of our artillery at it. But outside the pilot team, everybody has a queue of tasks to do."

Johnny jumps in. "Actually, as ironic as it might be, we are probably operating in very similar fashion to a shared services function. Well, at least we used to, before the pilot. We break every case into small tasks, we assign them to individuals . . ."

Mary instinctively picks up Johnny's thread. "We track completion, check quality—my goodness, you're right!"

"So, just to summarize," Jerry ruminates, "if we go back to

the old way of doing things, we basically make the argument for Elrod. But if we go all in with the Mojo Squad model, we will be very exposed in the short run, because our backlog will likely go through the roof. We are stuck between a rock and a hard place."

He pauses for a second and then thinks about Cameron's state trooper story. "Well, I think we should go all in, full speed. We know it's the better way; we just don't have the data yet to prove it. Are you in?"

Both of them nod. "All in, boss. The last few months have been a blast." Johnny exclaims.

"Great! Let's get right to it. By the way, we should check with Eric and Dakota since they signed up for creating a plan."

"They make a strange pair," Mary comments. "I am really curious what they will come up with."

"Well, probably nothing yet," adds Johnny. "I mean, the staff meeting was only two weeks ago."

"I wouldn't be so sure about that," Jerry cautions. "Lately, I've seen some of our team do some pretty amazing things already in this process. So, let's find out. Do you think we can get them to join us for a few minutes?"

Johnny disappears to go looking for Eric and Dakota.

While he is out, Mary and Jerry start to put together a plan for collecting data that will help them make their point. Mary wants to go back through the old productivity reports to create a baseline. "But how do we track whether the new process is faster?"

Jerry ponders her question for a while. Then he has an epiphany. "How about we ask the Mojo Squad, Mary? They are the ones closest to the work."

Mary agrees.

Johnny returns with Eric and Dakota in tow.

"Thanks for joining us," Jerry welcomes them. "Hey, I know we just had the department meeting, but we were wondering—"

Before Jerry can complete the sentence, Eric announces. "Jerry, we have a draft plan." He motions for Dakota to continue.

Dakota is visibly nervous but presses forward. "We think it would take us half a year to get everybody up to speed on the various tools, assuming we copy what the Mojo Squad has been doing. I have met with them twice now. Now, that is a somewhat conservative estimate, because I also talked to Meredith. She has been here about a month but already seems very comfortable with straightforward cases, so maybe it will take less. The biggest issue will be how exactly to phase this in."

Eric further clarifies the dilemma. "The main challenge, Jerry, is how we move from our current way of working, where every case is broken down into a bunch of tasks that are assigned in a somewhat random manner"—his words elicit a frown on Mary's face as he continues the thought—"to everybody working on the same case. But we think we can handle that. Now what that will do to the backlog?" Eric shrugs his shoulders. "I guess that remains to be seen."

Jerry jumps in. "Don't worry about the backlog. So, how quickly do you think we can turn this on?"

Eric and Dakota look at each other. Then Eric responds, "The soonest we could do this would be four weeks. That gives us barely enough time to sort through the transitions and do some basic training."

Johnny perks up. "What if we were to align each pod to a sales region. Would that help?"

Eric thinks for a few seconds. "I think that would help a ton, Johnny. Good idea."

Johnny smiles.

Jerry affirms, "I like it. I already talked to Bellamy, and he is certainly rooting for us, so we should be okay with Sales, but I will need to manage their expectations. Looks like we will have a rough couple of months initially, before things get better, but I think I can sell that things will indeed get a lot better. And obviously I will need to talk to Cameron. But let's assume he buys in. Let's do it!"

Everybody looks at him.

"You are sure, Jerry?" Mary asks.

Jerry smiles. "Yes, I am sure. We need more Mojo Squads, and we need them now!"

Everybody laughs.

Accordingly, Eric and Dakota commit to producing a detailed plan by the end of the week, before heading back to their desks.

Jerry summarizes the various action items and decisions. "So, we will launch across the board on June first. We will try to align the pods to the sales teams. Mary, you will reach out to the Mojo Squad to figure out how to track our productivity, so we can make the case. Dakota and Eric will produce a training plan by next week. What are we missing?"

Johnny is the first to respond. "Well, how do we put those teams together?"

Mary nods. "I was thinking the same thing. Plus, where do we fit in?"

Jerry looks at her. "What do you mean, Mary?"

She sighs. "Well, Jerry, who will manage all these pods?"

Jerry thinks for a few seconds, before responding. "Well, do we need supervisors? From what I can see, the pods will be perfectly able to sort out who does what."

The moment he says that he regrets it. Both Mary and Johnny are clearly stunned, and justifiably so. He just challenged their livelihood, and that is not his intention.

"Mary and Johnny, just to be clear—you are both irreplaceable, but I think there are so many other ways we can leverage your skills and expertise beyond case scheduling and quality reviews."

Silence. But then Johnny nods. "I agree. I mean, the teams need coaching, but I don't think they need much else. I mean, they figured out how to manage the work, and quite frankly even the training. This is all new, so in effect they have had to train themselves as they process cases."

Jerry thinks back unnervingly to his last conversation with Cuthbert. Could he, in fact, do without supervisors? He thinks of the implications. He would have to do fifteen performance reviews instead of three. That sucked. But was it even possible? He asks the obvious yet loaded question:

"So, what will the two of you do?"

They both look at each other. Johnny shrugs. "I could help with coaching. If everybody here is going to be talking to the customers, they will need a lot of training—and some of them will need to go to charm school!"

Jerry laughs.

Then Mary speaks up. "Well, if Johnny teaches charm school, maybe I would like to work on improving our systems. I've been following what Tatum has been doing with those robots, and I think we can take that further."

This was unexpected. "Well, let's cross that bridge when we get there. We have plenty of work coming up that needs to be supervised. But we need to talk about the other point you raised. How will we put together those teams?"

They start to talk about personalities and skills but quickly realize they are going down a rabbit hole. Mary offers to put together a proposal for how to deploy the teams, which Jerry quickly accepts. Before they leave, they decide to schedule a departmental meeting in three weeks to review that plan.

As they leave the room, Johnny taps Jerry on his shoulder. "Bold move, Jerry. I did not think you were as brave as you are."

Jerry smiles. "Well, what else can we do? Roll over and play dead?"

Everybody laughs.

22

DOUBLING DOWN

Time really does fly, Jerry thinks, as he pulls into the Cons parking lot. He marvels at what his department has accomplished over the past three weeks. Dakota and Eric had laid out a thorough training schedule. And after much back and forth, Mary and Johnny had developed a proposal for staffing the pods.

There had been a lot of discussion about where to put Tatum, as they felt that each of the pods could greatly benefit from his tech skills. Mary had convinced them that if they really thought he could add so much value, why not make his main job to support everybody else but not work directly on specific cases himself—at least for the time being? Jerry now thinks this was quite an elegant solution.

So they had settled on four pods. They had also decided to break up the Mojo Squad so that they could have one person in each pod who had been part of the initial pilot. That decision yields some interesting pairings.

The first pod is Ryan, Skylar, and Rasheed. The second pod is Eric, Dakota, and Michele. Long an enigma to Jerry, Eric had since revealed himself as somebody who deeply cared about his work—enough so that Jerry has faith that Eric will grow to anchor the second pod. The third pod is Hannah, Meredith, and Olivia. Leaving Lee and Tatum for the fourth pod, Mary had proposed she also join that pod, which would allow her to work closely with Tatum on automation. Jerry remains unsure about Lee, because he had seemed quite disengaged over the last couple of months. But he figures, hey, that will be Mary's problem to sort out.

That had left Johnny as his second in command and lead trainer. Johnny is visibly energized by the assignment—he had been chomping at the bit for weeks to tell everybody about his new focus. Jerry had to remind him on a daily basis to keep his mouth shut.

Relying on Mary and Johnny to work out the details, Jerry began working on pitching the plan to Cameron and Bellamy. Selling Cameron on the idea had been surprisingly easy, though largely because he seems preoccupied with customer service issues. Thankfully none of those seemed to be the result of the still enormous backlog the onboarding team was juggling. When Jerry explains to him the concept of pods that would take a case from start to finish, he nods absentmindedly—and proceeds to complain to Jerry about turnover.

"Jerry, I am at my wit's end," Cameron laments. "Last month we had nine resignations in the call center. Nine! The whole group is about eighty, so what is that on an annual basis?"

Jerry does some quick math in his head. "Nine times twelve is 108, so something like 125 percent?"

"Exactly! It takes us six months to train them and get them up to speed, and we lose them after a year. We put in a request for two additional trainers, just so we can try to keep up! And of course, we did not budget for that."

After the Northpoint success, getting Bellamy on board had been easy as well. As Jerry had explained the proposed pod concept, Bellamy became clearly delighted that each of the pods would be aligned to a specific sales leader. Somewhat concerned about Jerry's plan to break up the Mojo Squad, Bellamy had ultimately agreed with his rationale.

"The sales guys will be delighted; I can promise you that," Bellamy had beamed. "Shelley has been telling everyone how quickly you guys can turn around cases. So, the bar is set high."

Jerry had reminded Bellamy to make sure that all the sales teams, as well as the brokers, knew that the onboarding team needed to work directly with their clients. "Don't you worry about that, Jerry. I told them. And then I had Shelley repeat it."

Jerry had been stunned, stammering, "Y-You already did that?"

But Bellamy had only laughed. "Yes, I did. So now all your team needs to do is to let the salespeople know when to set up the first call." He had looked at Jerry. "Whenever you are ready. You tell me. But we are good to go on our end. And everybody is rooting for you, Jerry!"

After wrapping up that meeting, Jerry had felt the pressure of rolling things out too fast. *Speed kills*, he pondered. Still, he had left the meeting with Bellamy feeling a good bit taller.

———————

Unfortunately—and most ironically—the next departmental meeting does not go quite as smoothly as Jerry might have anticipated or hoped for. Although Jerry, Mary, and Johnny had tried to anticipate every possible reaction to the decision to move to pods, from the moment the meeting opens they quickly realize that their proposal is making some team members visibly uncomfortable.

For starters, Hannah expresses her frustration in trying to understand who is going to assign her what cases to work on. When Johnny explains that each pod will decide who does what, she responds with sarcasm. "You want us to figure that out? So what do you get paid for?" Jerry sighs.

Rasheed also expresses some concerns. He is rather vague at first, but it soon becomes apparent that his real concern is whether he might have to stay beyond 5:00 p.m. from time to time. He finally admits that he must be on time for rehearsals with his band. When Jerry assures him that they will accommodate his schedule, Rasheed seems relieved. Jerry cannot help but note the decidedly non-career-minded nature of Rasheed's main concern, at least as it might apply to his career with Consolidated Insurance. He sighs again.

Lee also seems unhappy, though he is difficult to read, because he sits there not saying anything. *Well, there are always the skeptics*, Jerry thinks.

Jerry explains how Johnny will support the teams and provide training and coaching, and that Mary and Tatum would look at additional automation opportunities. "I know we are moving fast, but I think the pilot has demonstrated this concept can work. Each pod will own their cases from start to finish. We stand ready to support you, but you will have a lot of autonomy here. And you will be aligned to a sales team, which should help with communications." He reminds them of the feedback they received from Northpoint. "The clients clearly like this new way of working. And from what I see from the pilot team, those who do the work like it better, too."

Ryan and Michele give him a thumbs-up, and Olivia nods.

"I know this will be a change, and change is hard. We will track this closely. If you run into any problems please let Mary, Johnny, or me know." Jerry pauses. "Thank you for your support and trust."

After the meeting, Jerry spends a few minutes catching up with Mary. She walks him through what she has done to create a baseline. "We decided to look at the entire last year, looking at weekly caseload, cycle time, percentage of cases that went live on day one, and the number of customer service calls that can be directly tied to missing the go-live date."

Jerry is impressed. "How did you manage to get all that data?"

Mary smiles. "Well, Tatum is not only an expert on bots. He was able to mine the customer service data using some tool he has. Within a day he had it all sorted out."

"Did Customer Service agree to this?"

"Well, I talked to Ava. She was complaining about the difficulty in training her teams. So I proposed Johnny run a few sessions on onboarding issues in exchange for letting Tatum dig into her data."

"And she agreed to that?"

"She loved the idea," Mary says assuredly. "Johnny did a great job, by the way, and I think the training will pay dividends. Now at least some of the Customer Service people know what we are doing and how to address issues when something falls through the cracks."

Jerry is delighted to see the initiative, although he worries a bit about not being kept in the loop. But he also knows he can trust his team. Well, at least Mary and Johnny.

Jerry looks closer at the charts Mary put in front of him. "Okay, I get it; this is the baseline. Looks like we suck!"

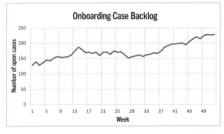

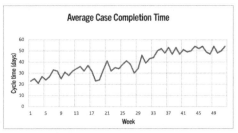

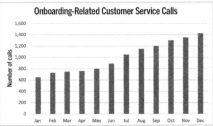

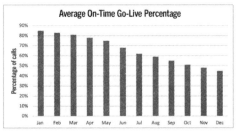

Mary points out the pattern: the higher the backlog, the longer the cycle time. And the longer the case takes, the less likely they are to make the go-live date. Subsequently, as they increasingly fail to hit the go-live date, the result is a dramatic increase in customer service calls.

"I mean, it makes intuitive sense," Jerry states, "but to see it right in front of you . . . this is powerful. But how are we doing this year? And can we see the impact of the pilot yet?"

Mary smiles. "I knew that you would ask that. So here is the picture for this year." And she pulls out another set of charts.

Jerry studies the charts. The gray lines and bars indicate their current year totals, while the black lines and bars represent their previous year. He looks at Mary. "Okay, so we still suck. I knew it would take a while for the pilot to show results, but I was hoping we would see at least some improvement. I mean, we got rid of the sales reports, and that was supposed to free up time to knock down the backlog."

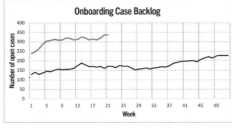

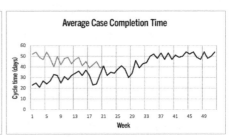

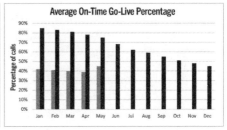

Mary reminds him that they started the pilot only a couple of weeks ago. "It will take a while to show up on this report, Jerry, but here is something you will probably find helpful." And with that, she pulls out a final chart.

"These are the numbers for the pilot team. I excluded Northpoint since we picked that up halfway through the process. So, these are the numbers for the new National Accounts cases we have processed so far."

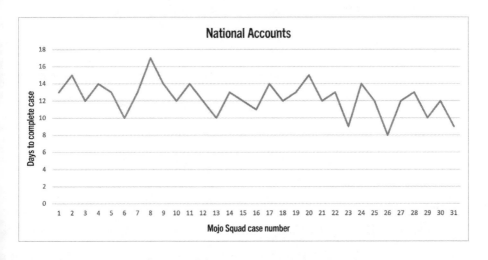

Jerry looks at the chart. *This can't be right*, he thinks. "Mary, are you sure about this? I do recall the first case went through really quickly, but I assumed that was the result of the team starting without a backlog of cases."

"Yes, Jerry, that clearly helped. Not having a huge caseload definitely helped avoid some of the constant reshuffling we so often need to do to accommodate whoever screams the loudest. I checked the numbers three times, and I even asked Ryan to check them against their whiteboard. These numbers are accurate," Mary states confidently.

Son of a gun, Jerry thinks. Cycle times this year had been ranging from forty to sixty-five days, looking at the weekly averages. And he reminds himself that these are averages. But how could the team get the cases through the system so quickly?

"Is this right? Eight days?" Jerry points at case number 26.

Mary grins. "Yes, Jerry, it is true. Being able to talk to the customer has been a game changer."

That is the understatement of the day, Jerry thinks. "This is awesome, Mary. Please keep updating these charts. They will come in handy *if* we have to make the case against a shared service model."

As Mary agrees and departs, Jerry realizes that *if* might very likely become *when*.

UP AND RUNNING

Given how much effort has gone into planning the cutover to the new model, Jerry expects the first days to be marked by chaos and confusion. But somehow, they manage to pull it off without any major problems.

Not surprisingly, there is some frustration when the team realizes that not all the sales reps had gotten the memo that Jerry's teams were now empowered to talk to customers. And when Tatum's life product robot stops working only a week into the new workflow, the snafu causes a minor panic. But they quickly figure out the issue and soon they are back on track.

There are the inevitable internal complaints, most of them coming from Hannah, who seems to require a lot of hand-holding. But her pod-mates Olivia and Meredith do their best to talk her off the ledge. *Some people just have a little difficulty with change*, thinks Jerry.

Eventually, however, all four pods are up and running, each with their own whiteboard for daily stand-ups and workload management. Jerry is reminded of a Yogi Berra quote he once heard: "You can observe a lot by just watching." So true.

Jerry can tell how each team is doing by simply looking at their boards.

Two of the pods had gotten off to a slow start, not unexpectedly, being weighed down as they were by the large preexisting backlog. Although fortunately, they had been proactive in conferring with Sales to push out, by an extra month, the go-live date on some of the most complex cases, which helped enormously—at least in the short run. With the pods being able to concentrate on the less complex cases, Jerry could see the caseload steadily dropping. Not as quickly as he would have liked, but they had at least started to make a dent. *Rome was not built in a day*, Jerry reminds himself.

As things progress, Jerry finds it fascinating to see how each pod develops a unique approach for getting the work done. He had assumed that they would simply copy and paste the workflow the pilot pod had established. But Ryan had convinced him otherwise.

"We can propose it as a starting point," Ryan had argued, "but they need to figure out what works best for them." What a smart and effective idea.

When, at one point, Hannah and Lee had complained about certain aspects of the draft process flow Michele had created to help her colleagues, Ryan had suggested almost blithely that they do whatever works best for their pod. "There is no shortage of good ideas, so I am looking forward to seeing what you come up with," Ryan had counseled, and that had seemed almost miraculously to quiet the criticism.

And while he is still waiting on Mary to update the charts she shared a while back, Jerry can see some early signs. At long last, they are starting to reduce the case backlog. He had asked the teams to track the time to complete a case on their whiteboards, and so far everybody's numbers are trending down. Jerry also notices how much less effort seems to be required to track cases and assign tasks. Wow, progress!

And on top of that, Bob has found a few candidates for the second open role. This time, Jerry really enjoys the job interview process. Funny how easy it is to fill a role if it's a good job!

This time around, Jerry starts off each interview by asking the candidates about the best job and the worst job they have ever had. He then explains that at Cons, they have made an effort to create good, intrinsically rewarding jobs. "We are organized in small pods, each of them handling a case from start to finish. The teams organize themselves and coordinate directly with each of the clients they serve. We are investing in robotics to get rid of repetitive tasks. This is a very important part of the customer experience and critical for our success; if we mess up, the first impression is ruined."

Judging from the candidates' responses, this dynamic pitch works wonders. All three express strong interest to join the team. It's a difficult choice, but after the interviews are completed, Jerry asks Bob to extend an offer to Roheela.

"What about the others?" Bob poses, suggesting Jerry select a second candidate in case Roheela turns them down.

"I am pretty sure she will take the job, Bob," Jerry replies, somewhat surprised at his own innate optimism about this one, "but okay, second choice is Cheryl."

The result comes swiftly; before the day is over, Bob calls back to tell him that Roheela accepted the offer.

Jerry smiles. "Thanks for the update—and for all your help."

"My pleasure, Jerry. Oh, and by the way," Bob pauses for a

few seconds, "I don't know what you did differently this time, but those three were all eager to join your team. How did you manage to sell them?"

Jerry suppresses a laugh. "Bob, you can only do a good job if there is a good job to be done. And we just made an effort to turn these crappy jobs into real good ones. You should come down here sometime; I can show you what we did."

"Sounds interesting. I will drop in over the next few days. Oh, and before I forget, we should also talk about the supervisor role—you know, backfilling for Julia. The req has been approved!"

Jerry thinks to himself, *What a joke!*

Bob continues, "Any ideas where you want to post this job? Also, we need to list this internally in case we have some qualified candidates in-house."

He realizes that he never told Bob that they had gotten rid of the supervisors. Okay, they had not eliminated the role but instead found a better use for Mary's and Johnny's skills. And so far, it seems the pods are perfectly capable of figuring out what to do, when to do it, and how to get it done.

So, thinking quickly, while knowing he really does not need another supervisor, Jerry realizes he's got an ace in the hole. "Bob, thanks for the reminder. Can you hold off on that for now? I need to sort out a few things first, but I promise, I will get back to you before the end of the week."

"No worries, Jerry. I have plenty of work over here. Just wanted to let you know. You tell me when you want to pull the trigger on this."

"Sure will, Bob. And again, thanks for all your help." Jerry hangs up and makes a note on his whiteboard to discuss the topic with Mary and Johnny.

As he sits back down, he notices on his computer screen a meeting invitation from Ben, with the title "Project Sunrise." What the heck was Project Sunrise? The new claims system? Or is it the shared services effort Ben had mentioned to him?

Jerry scans the meeting invite for clues. Besides himself and Ava, the head of Customer Service, it lists Gordon; Ben; Cameron; Richard, the chief financial officer; Colleen, the head of HR; and Mark, who heads up Procurement. And of course, his friend Elrod.

Okay, so Project Sunrise is the code name for the shared services boondoggle, Jerry surmises. He had been wondering what was going on with that. The meeting is scheduled for this coming Friday at 4:00 p.m. That means he can forget about leaving the office early to get a head start on traffic. But it will give Mary enough time to update the data she had presented to him in May. Armed with the facts, Jerry believes he should be able to convince them to leave him alone.

He wonders how Cuthbert would approach this, which makes him realize it has been almost three months since they caught up. Jerry grabs his phone and sends him a quick text, asking Cuthbert whether he has some time to meet over the next few days. He is surprised to get a nearly immediate response. Cuthbert proposes they meet Friday morning for a coffee, if Jerry is available. He checks his calendar, moves a few things around to free up his schedule, and confirms.

24

WISDOM PEARLS

As Jerry pulls into the parking lot of the bakery where he and Cuthbert first ran into each other at the start of the year, he sees that Cuthbert has already grabbed one of the few outdoor tables. Approaching the table, Jerry notices a cup of coffee already waiting for him.

"Jerry, I took the liberty of ordering for you. Hope coffee black is good?"

"Perfect, Mike. And thank you."

"No worries, buddy. I figured I'd save us some time. I need to dart off in an hour to meet some investors, but I've been looking forward to this. How are things?"

It takes Jerry a while to bring Cuthbert up to speed, so much has happened. When he mentions that they changed the role of the supervisors, Cuthbert is visibly intrigued. "Wow, Jerry, I am proud of you. That is a bold move."

Jerry nods. "Yes, I was nervous about that, too. But it went off without a hitch." He finishes with sharing the latest statistics Mary has pulled together. "Well, our backlog is still somewhat high, but the time we need to implement a case has plummeted, Mike. I mean, we are still early stages, but each of the pods is seeing great reductions in cycle time."

Cuthbert smiles. "I'd like to say I'm surprised, but I'm not. This is great to hear."

Jerry then moves on to talk about Project Sunrise, and the meeting scheduled for later in the day. When he is done, Cuthbert shakes his head. "Wow, that is messed up. Just as you are turning the corner, the wind is changing. So what is your plan?"

"Well," Jerry musters, "we have been collecting some of the stats. I hope that what we have is sufficient to make our case. What do you think?"

Cuthbert takes another sip of coffee. "If I were the CEO, this meeting wouldn't even happen. But from what you've told me about your company, you are right to be nervous. Common sense is rare these days. And in my experience, the higher up the food chain folks sit, the less idea they have of just how revolutionary what you are creating actually is." He pauses and then asks, "Are your friends from Sales invited?"

"No, they are not."

Pausing again, Cuthbert then offers, "Well, it would be awkward if you ask them to participate, since it is not your meeting. But you might want to share your stats with them."

Jerry nods. "Good idea. Any other thoughts?"

Cuthbert sighs. "To be honest, Jerry, I can see this going either way. You definitely have a strong case. And I am sure most of your people love the new setup."

"They sure do," Jerry affirms. "Even the naysayers are on board. Well, for the most part."

Cuthbert nods. "I'm not surprised. Owning the work is a powerful motivator. It sounds like you've given them a lot of autonomy. Can they tell how they are doing?"

Jerry nods.

"Well, then you've succeeded! Okay, nicely done. You are on the road to success," Cuthbert states.

Jerry looks at his watch. "Mike, I know you need to run, but do you have any last words of wisdom?"

Cuthbert chuckles. "Words of wisdom? Well, I'm not sure about that. But," he pauses to take a last sip of coffee, "the customer is always right. Right?"

Jerry listens and processes.

"Sorry, but I really do have to go," Cuthbert says as he gets up from the table. "I am sure you will be fine. Text me to let me know how the meeting goes. I'm curious and I can't wait to hear."

"Will do," Jerry replies. "Thanks so much. Really, for everything."

"Good luck, Jerry."

Jerry shortly departs as well and heads to the office. The first thing Jerry does when he arrives is call Bellamy, only to get his voicemail. He leaves a message asking Bellamy to call him back but doesn't hear back from him before he heads to the meeting.

ROUND ONE

If Jerry had been impressed with the elegance of Bellamy's office, he is flabbergasted by the opulence of the rosewood-paneled boardroom on this, his first-ever visit to the top-floor suite. Standing in the corner is a fancy espresso machine that Jerry surmises to be no cheap knockoff. It looks like it could have been airlifted from one of those picturesque Italian bistros that Jerry and Haley had fallen in love with during their first trip abroad. Hard to believe that had been at least five years ago now.

But there is little time for romantic reverie, because Jerry is not the first one to arrive. Ben and Cameron are already there, chatting furtively, or so it appears to Jerry. Colleen is trying to figure out how to get the espresso maker to work. She gives up and walks over to Jerry. "Hey, Jer, how's life?"

Jerry had met Colleen only twice before—and he hates it when people shorten his name. His dad had been adamant about reminding everybody that his name was Thomas. Not Tom or Tommy. Thomas. But this was not the time to make new enemies. "Very well, Colleen. Oh, and before I forget, Bob has been really helpful. He—"

Before he can finish his sentence, Elrod, Gordon, Richard, and Mark enter the room. Gordon heads to his seat at the head of the table. "Sorry for the late meeting, folks, but I hope to get you out of here in no time. Let's get started."

Jerry has previously met Gordon only a handful of times. He knows that Gordon is an actuary by training, although that had been a long time ago. And these days he definitely does not come across as one. His demeanor reminds Jerry of Bellamy—all smiles, affable, if only slightly sterner, perhaps as a requirement of his position at the top. Jerry snags a seat next to Cameron.

Ava, the head of Customer Service, enters the room. "Am I late?" Everybody turns to her. Jerry looks at his watch. *Yes, you are*, he thinks to himself.

Gordon smiles. "Ava, you are right on time. Grab a seat, and let's go. Elrod, do you want to kick us off?"

Elrod, who grabbed a seat to the right of Gordon, grins. "Happy to do so. Folks, before we get started," Elrod pauses, "I would like to ask you to keep what we discuss strictly confidential." As he is saying that Jerry realizes that Elrod is looking at Ben.

Elrod continues. "Some of you are already aware of this, but for the rest of you . . ."—Elrod looks at Ava and then Jerry and Cameron—"this might be news." A more dramatic pause. "Project Sunrise. That is the name of our shared services initiative, which will propel Cons into the twenty-first century."

Elrod fires up his laptop and starts going through his slide deck. "You all know that we are facing some real profitability challenges this year. Ben and I have been thinking about how we can close our profit gap. And the answer we have come up with is shared services." Elrod pauses again for dramatic effect and then continues. "A lot of our administrative workforce is managed suboptimally. We intend to change that."

He pushes a button on his laptop, and an organizational chart appears on the screen. He pushes it again, and red circles magically appear on the chart, highlighting Customer Service, Onboarding, Human Resources, and Procurement. "We have been talking with some consultants, and their analysis suggests that we would greatly benefit from pulling all the transactional work into a shared services center."

Taking a breath, Elrod continues. "We estimate that we have approximately 120 employees that should be moved into a shared services center. That will free up your teams to focus on the work that matters." He looks at Colleen from HR and Mark from Procurement.

And then his gaze moves to Cameron. "And Cameron, this will of course be most relevant for your teams. I'd like you to just think about the efficiencies we can gain." He pushes the button again. A bunch of numbers appear on the screen. "Looking at the benchmarks, we think we can turn this into a net impact of $7 million. And let me remind you, that would be a net profit increase of 20 percent." Elrod glances at Gordon. "I assume you would be interested in that?"

Gordon laughs. "You bet I am! Keep going!"

Jerry cannot help but think that they must have rehearsed this little dog and pony show. Elrod continues, "Our consultants tell us that we should assume a 20 percent improvement in productivity and a 30 percent improvement in costs."

Cameron raises his hand. "Elrod, sorry to interrupt, but how did you come up with the cost estimates?"

Elrod flashes a toothy smile. "Cameron, thanks for the

question. The consultants ran the numbers. And as you can imagine, they have a lot of experience."

Jerry expects Cameron to fold, but his boss surprises him with his feisty response. "Okay, that is great, but please explain to me how we can cut everybody's pay by 30 percent?"

Jerry looks around the room. Everybody is looking at Elrod, who is still smiling, as he responds. "Well, Cameron, the model assumes that half the benefits will come from economies of scale. And the other half will come from replacing our current, very expensive employees with new ones who are paid more in line with market rates."

And before anybody can say anything, Gordon interjects. "Elrod, great presentation. Makes a lot of sense to me. And I can tell you, our shareholders will love this." The room falls silent for a minute.

Jerry realizes that now is the time to speak up. Now or never. He clears his throat. "Elrod?" He and Elrod lock eyes. "That is a very interesting proposition. But have you thought about or anticipated the impact on our customers?"

Elrod is clearly not happy with Jerry raining on his parade. "Well, they will be happy, too. We will implement a state-of-the-art ticketing system to avoid the issues you all are struggling with." Now he looks directly at Jerry. "I know your team has been having a hard time keeping up with the workload, but I think we can fix that issue quickly." He then glances at Gordon. "I am sure you want to see the timeline for this project?"

But before Gordon can answer, Jerry pipes up again. "Well, Elrod, I don't think you are aware of some of the changes we have been making. We're actually going the other way, putting fragmented workflows back together, and the results—"

But before he can finish his point, Elrod cuts him off. "I know what you've been up to, Jerry. But I happen to think that there's got to be a better way than installing untested software. We both know that your bots should have been cleared by the security team."

Gordon is leaning forward. "Hold on, Elrod. Do we have a security issue? And what is a bot?"

Jerry stares first at Elrod and then at Ben, who is avoiding eye contact. *Holy crap*, he thinks. *So this is how the sausage got made.*

Elrod turns around to face Gordon directly. "Jerry and his team have been implementing some robotics software. I am sure it was all with good intentions. But according to our cyber security guidelines—which by the way you all signed off on last year—that is not how it's supposed to work."

Jerry is stunned. He had been prepared to talk about the changes they have been implementing and the difference those changes have already made, but none of that seems to matter at this point in time. His mind is racing.

Just then, Cameron chimes in. "Elrod, Gordon, I am so sorry. That is my fault. I told Jerry to go ahead."

Jerry is flummoxed. Mr. Sunny-Side Up coming to his rescue?

Cameron continues, first looking at Jerry then the others as he says rather benignly, "But you two might recall that you told us we should not expect any help at all, given that everyone in your shop is so focused on the claims project." Cameron now pauses for dramatic effect. "Which makes me wonder, why are we talking about shared services. Did you guys give up on 'revolutionizing claims'?" Everybody in the room picks up on the sarcasm in his voice.

Jerry thinks to himself, this is a "mic drop" moment. He had not expected Cameron to go to bat for him, let alone poke Elrod right in the eyes. But here it is—Cameron at the plate—and it emboldens Jerry to jump back into the fray.

"Elrod," Jerry begins calmly, mindful to look as "executive" as he can muster in the moment, "I just want to make sure you understand all the facts. We are making some important process changes we think have great potential to improve the customer experience."

For a nanosecond, Jerry wonders whether he should talk about the "good jobs" concept, but he intuits that might be a step too far for the people in this room. He presses ahead. "Sales is fully on board with this, and we have just radically changed how we are organized. Instead of everybody just doing bits and bobs of the work, we now have teams of three that take a case from start to finish. They are now talking directly to the customer, which has helped us to significantly reduce our turnaround times. And we think it will also greatly reduce the number of calls related to onboarding issues Ava and her Customer Service team are getting on their end. Each onboarding team is connected to their counterparts in Sales, so Sales know exactly who they can go to if there is an issue."

Jerry pauses, takes a quiet breath. Okay, time to go all in. "Bellamy is very excited about the changes we are making, and I really think you should get his input on this."

Gordon has stopped smiling and now stares at Jerry, who continues. "Of course, efficiency and cost are important, but we also need to make sure our customers are happy."

Before Elrod can respond, Gordon chimes in. "Of course, the customer comes first. Elrod, why don't you talk to Bellamy about this?"

But Elrod is not ready to give up. "Gordon, I will, but I doubt it will change the recommendations. What we propose is based on industry best practices."

Jerry sees an opening, albeit a narrow one. "Gordon, are you familiar with Northpoint?" Gordon seems surprised, thinks for a moment, but responds eventually. "Yes, of course, that was a big win. A miracle, actually, given how pissed off they were the last time around."

Jerry nods. "Exactly. A miracle. Ask Bellamy. He can tell you the whole story. The changes we made were crucial to deliver on Northpoint, and now we are leveraging that model across the entire department." He turns to Elrod. "Elrod, the changes we made allow us to turn around cases in less than three weeks. Now, I'm sure you and your consulting team did a great job running all those numbers. But I think you need to consider that our customers care for the end-to-end experience. If we follow your recommendations, we will go to an even more fragmented workflow than we have today. Instead of the enrollment process taking six or seven people, it will take fifteen."

Before Elrod can respond, Cameron jumps in. "Jerry, thanks for keeping us focused on what matters—the customer! And Elrod, I love the initiative, but we've been thinking along similar lines with regards to Customer Service. Maybe we can hold off on this until we see if what we are doing works?"

Elrod seems a bit at a loss. Then Ben jumps in. "I have to agree with Cameron and Jerry. We are getting our ass kicked in the marketplace, so making our customers happy comes first. But Jerry, we would love to see some data that backs up your improvement claims. And maybe we should include Bellamy in this conversation?"

Gordon looks at his watch. He says hurriedly, "Well, folks, looks like we have some sort of next steps. Let's definitely include Bellamy in our next meeting. Oh, and thank you Elrod and Ben for getting us started." He grins. "Okay, folks, I'm sorry but I'm gonna be late for a round of golf with our esteemed state senator if I don't get out of here in the next five minutes. Anything else we need to talk about?"

Jerry glances at Elrod, who seems to be biting his tongue.

"Great, so let's reconvene next week," Gordon states abruptly, closing his portfolio, and adding, "and Elrod, maybe next time we try for a better time? Traffic this time of day is a bitch—especially on a Friday!"

Everybody laughs, although Jerry can see Colleen taking notice. You can't use words like "bitch" anymore—at least not in the boardroom.

A short while later as Jerry sits in traffic on his way home, he plays the meeting back in his mind. He thought it went reasonably well, but did it really? He is no longer so sure. Jerry wonders what Elrod took away from that meeting. There would of course be a "round two," Jerry predicts. But hopefully he can enlist Bellamy's support. At that moment, Jerry's phone vibrates with an incoming call. Ha! It's Bellamy. What a strange coincidence.

"Jerry here," he answers on speakerphone.

"Bellamy there! How are you, buddy?" Bellamy starts with surprising energy.

"Okay, I guess. We just finished a meeting on—"

"—creating a shared services organization to save a few bucks," Bellamy says. "I know."

Jerry can't hold back a chuckle. "Who told you?"

"Gordon called me. From the golf course, ten minutes ago, the son of a gun. We talked about the revenue forecast. And then he asked about you."

"Me? What did you say?"

Bellamy chuckles. "I told him that you are a good guy, and that you are somebody who actually gives a damn. And that you did a great job selling me on your pilot. And that it seems to work." He pauses. "I might also have told him that we just decided to turn our new way of doing business into a formal service offering! We are even printing up brochures. Hey, Jerry, could I get some of your guys to pose for a picture? But only send the good-looking ones!" Bellamy laughs wickedly.

"Bellamy, you are a trip," Jerry replies, seeing the traffic starting to move better. "Hey, Bellamy?"

"Yes, Jerry?"

"I hope you're not upset that I used your name. But I think this little thing we started—"

Bellamy completes his sentence for him: "—will make a huge difference to a lot of people who otherwise would waste their precious time complaining to their employers about how they could not get the benefits they pay for out of each paycheck. Then the employer complains to the broker, and when the broker gets pissed off, we don't get to play, and so on."

Jerry is impressed. Bellamy has been paying attention.

"I told him all that," Bellamy insists. "You are on to something there, my friend. All the sales reps are talking about this—and they like it. The brokers like it. The clients like it. It even looks like your guys like it! What is there not to like? I can't believe nobody thought of this before."

Jerry is intently listening, feeling unexpectedly validated.

Bellamy continues, "I told Gordon how important it is—what you are doing. And that we just informed all the sales guys that they have dedicated teams working directly for them. Teams that will be talking directly to their customers to get all that admin stuff sorted out—so that they don't have to get tangled up in that anymore. And that we told the same story to the brokers."

"Wow, that's amazing," Jerry utters; it's about all he can muster in the moment, his eyes glued to the crowded highway.

"Anyway, I think Gordon got it. I think you and your crew will be okay," Bellamy declares and then laughs. "Oh, and Jerry, don't forget to let me know when we can take those pictures for the brochure, okay? Enjoy the weekend, buddy. Gotta go!" And before Jerry can even respond, he hangs up.

Jerry decides that Bellamy had been joking when he asked about putting photographs of his team into some sort of brochure. But the more important piece of news, of course, was that Gordon had reached out to Bellamy. That was probably a very good sign.

A loud honk reminds Jerry to focus on the job at hand—getting home. By the time he gets there, it's 7:30 p.m., all thanks to Elrod and his late Friday meeting. As he gets out of the car, Jerry's phone rings again. It's Cameron. Jerry is torn for a second. Let it go to voicemail? But then he remembers how things went down this afternoon. Cameron had really surprised him when he backed him up on the robots. He did not have to. Plus, Cameron was his boss. Plus, Jerry was curious to hear what Cameron thought of the meeting.

So, he picks up, standing in the driveway. "Jerry here!"

"Jerry, hey. I know it is late, but I was wondering if you have a few minutes to talk about that meeting earlier?"

"No worries, happy to," Jerry replies.

Then Cameron continues, "I was a bit surprised by Elrod's proposal. Ben told me a while back that they were looking at some shared services concepts, but I didn't realize it would include my entire department."

"Well, HR, Finance, and Procurement are apparently also included," Jerry consolingly interjects.

Cameron grunts. "Okay, sure. But it is only a few folks for them. The bulk would be from Client Services. Primarily you and Ava. But that is not the point I wanted to make."

"Cameron, I am sorry about the bot issue," Jerry offers. "I should have told you about that. Ben came to me about this a while back and I thought we had it all sorted out. He was going to send some security guys over to look at what we were doing and check things over, but they never came by. I didn't mean for you to take the hit."

Cameron laughs. "Oh, that? My pleasure. But no, that is not what I wanted to talk about either." He pauses as Jerry leans against his car and shifts the phone to his other ear, preparing to hear what's next.

"We need to get our ducks in a row," Cameron warns. "This was just round one. Gordon will want that $7 million."

Cameron is right, Jerry realizes, adding plaintively, "But Bellamy will back us up. I just talked to him."

"Jerry, I know these guys," Cameron responds. "Gordon and Richard are all about the numbers. And we are under a lot of pressure. They just missed the revenue target. The stock is not doing great, and so if Gordon can get $7 million from some-place, he will take it. He won't care where it came from."

Jerry sighs, listening.

"I am intrigued by your little experiment," Cameron switches topics. "Those pods you keep talking about. I think you, me, and Ava should have a strategy session to see how we can spin that. You game for that?"

"Of course, Cameron. Anytime."

"Great, I will set something up. Anyway, you did a great job today. We'll see how it all plays out. Have a great weekend. Oh, Jerry, just one more thing."

"Yes, Cameron?" Jerry responds, thinking, *Now who's imitating Steve Jobs?*

"Bellamy asked me whether I am okay with putting pictures of y'all into this brochure he wants to hand out; I told him I was okay with it. Okay, gotta go. Bye!" And before Jerry can respond, Cameron hangs up, with Jerry left wondering why all of a sudden people seem to keep doing that.

Maybe that brochure thing is for real, Jerry thinks, making his way inside at last.

Later that evening, he tells Haley all that happened. She shakes her head when he recaps the scene in the boardroom. "Sounds like a TV show. You should write this stuff down— would make a good movie."

Jerry laughs. And when he tells her about his subsequent conversations with Bellamy and Cameron, she declares that he has enough material for a series. Jerry suddenly remembers that he had promised to send Cuthbert an update. He punches out a short text: "Went okay today but there will be a round 2." He hits send. Then he adds a second text with a request: "Would love to pick your brain, lmk if you have time for a call."

PICTURE PERFECT

Johnny and Mary are already sitting in front of Jerry's desk when he arrives at work the following Monday morning.

"How did it go?" asks Johnny, mincing no words before Jerry can even say hello.

Jerry grins through a grimace. "Well, I think it went about as well as it could under the circumstances." He gives them a short summary of the meeting. When Jerry tells them about how Elrod had tried to ambush him with the robots, Johnny gets visibly annoyed.

"What a jerk!" Johnny declares.

Jerry sums it up by saying, "The savings Elrod is promising is our biggest problem. It will be hard to argue economies of scale and lower salaries." He adds, "Cameron wants to have a strategy session with me and Ava. Oh, I almost forgot. Bellamy wants to take pictures of the team for some crazy brochure he's putting together."

They both stare at him, clearly in shock. "You are joking, right?" Mary exclaims incredulously.

"Nope. I had the same reaction when he told me. But he also talked to Cameron about it."

She shakes her head. "Well, we can bring that up in the staff meeting this afternoon."

Mary and Johnny head back to their desks, and Jerry dials into Bellamy's weekly sales meeting—which goes really well.

Later that day, Jerry's departmental meeting is uneventful; that is, until Jerry brings up the photo session. Not everybody is a fan.

"Do we actually have to do that?" whines Dakota, who clearly is not.

"No, of course not. Nobody will be forced to be in the picture," Jerry reassures.

Skylar, on the other hand, is interested but inquires about the dress code. Rasheed asks if he can get a copy. "Hey, I need a new headshot anyway, for the band."

Jerry tries to move the discussion along. "Folks, I don't even know the details yet. But if anybody does not want their picture taken, please let me know. Send me an email. Now, can we move on? What I really want to talk about is how things are going."

They go around the room discussing status. Each pod has its own challenges. Ryan, Skylar, and Rasheed, whose pod took over the National Accounts cases, are struggling, largely because breaking up the original team has substantially increased their backlog. But Ryan remains confident they will be able to catch up in due course.

Eric, Dakota, and Michele report next. Their pod is aligned to Victor, the sales director for the East region, and his team. They too had started off with a huge backlog of nearly 112 cases, but Eric proudly declares that, to date, they have managed to get it down to eighty. "These last few weeks have been brutal. Being able to talk to the customers takes a lot of time—getting the hang of it, I mean. But we think we have figured out how to make those calls more efficient, and we've created a checklist. We'd be happy to share that."

Jerry really likes how the pods are figuring out what works best for them. There is clearly no shortage of good ideas, a fact he has relied on throughout this entire process.

Hannah, Meredith, and Olivia are next. They are supporting Marco, the sales director responsible for the Central region, and Jeffrey, who is responsible for the West. Both of these regions happen to be a lot smaller than the East but are nevertheless important. Jerry is pleasantly surprised to see Meredith give the update for the pod. "We have not been able to put much of a dent into our caseload," she explains, "but we have talked to most of the clients, who all seem receptive to the idea that we are trying to do something different that will make things better in the long run, and we are starting to see some light at the end of the tunnel."

Last to report is the pod for the South region, consisting of Lee, Tatum, and Mary. "We are also a bit behind," Mary admits, "but that is okay. Lee and I have been trying to free up Tatum a bit so he can build some new robots. And I am happy to announce that as of yesterday we automated the census checks."

That is welcome news. A census check, done manually, could take anywhere from fifteen minutes to two hours. "That is great news. Well done, Tatum," Jerry says, "and thank you both, Mary and Lee, for giving him the time to work on that. I know we need to get those cases out and it is tempting to just focus on that, but all these improvements will add up and pay big dividends in the long run."

Johnny is next, giving an update on the training plan. "I have some open slots, if anybody wants some coaching." He sees hands shooting up in the air, and the slots fill up quickly.

Jerry shares that Roheela has accepted their offer and will start in a few weeks. "And that's all the news fit to print," Jerry repeats his usual closing. "Thanks for your time."

When he checks his phone later in the day, he sees a text from Cuthbert: "Traveling but could have a short call later in the week. How about Friday, 8:00 a.m.?" Jerry quickly replies to confirm and makes sure to update his calendar.

Jerry also notices a couple of meeting invites in his inbox.

The first one is from Cameron. Strategy session is Wednesday afternoon.

The second invite is from Elrod. The next meeting for Project Sunrise is scheduled for Friday at eleven. Jerry checks the list of participants. Yes, Bellamy is included—as are a couple of other people whose names Jerry does not recognize. Maybe the consultants he saw in the cafeteria?

SHOW ME THE MONEY

ameron and Ava are talking about football when Jerry opens the door to the conference room. "No way Clemson will beat Alabama!" Cameron bellows. He loves his Crimson Tide. "Hey, Jerry! Come on in." Jerry settles into a chair.

"Right on time. So let's get right to it," Cameron urges as he leans forward. "We need to talk about how we want to respond to Elrod's proposal. I think we dodged a bullet last Friday, but this will obviously not go away. The CFO called me this morning asking for a confirmation of our head count, which suggests to me that they are running the numbers."

"Really? That's disturbing, isn't it?" Jerry asks.

"Sure, it is," Cameron states, "but seven million bucks in cost savings? Of course, it is tempting. And hey, maybe it is the right thing to do." He looks at Jerry. "Jerry, you clearly impressed Gordon with your speech on the customer. And I saw Bellamy on the attendee list, so that should help us. But we need more if we want to convince Gordon to drop this idea. Either of you have any ideas?"

Ava shakes her head. "Well, it is hard to argue against economies of scale, although I feel that adding Jerry's group and a few

Finance and HR people on top of the eighty in my group won't make that much of a difference."

Cameron and Jerry nod in agreement. Ava continues, "But what about hiring lower-cost workers?"

Jerry grimaces, adding, "Well, Cons pays above market, at least that's what Bob told me. And I don't see how he will be able to find people to do the same work for a third less—at least not in this country."

Cameron chimes in. "You are making a good point. Elrod did not mention it, but he is probably looking at offshoring. So even if he needs twice as many people to do the job, he will still come out ahead, given that the wages are so much lower in India or the Philippines."

Jerry scratches his head. "Well, I am not sure how to translate it into dollars and cents, but the changes we are implementing are making a real difference. We are seeing cases being completed in less than two weeks."

Ava is impressed. "Two weeks? Are you sure? You guys used to take three months!"

"You're right, but since we created these pods and started working directly with customers, the numbers have come down. I mean, we still have a huge backlog to work through, and we still have to do a lot of training, but we are definitely headed in the right direction."

Cameron nods. "Too bad it won't help us win the argument on the savings. You still have about the same head count."

Jerry thinks about that for a second. "Well, not really. We actually took out the supervisors."

Ava looks at Jerry in surprise. "You took out the supervisors? How does that work?"

"It actually works great. Mary and Johnny are still there, of course, but Johnny is now focused on training and coaching, which he loves. And Mary is working cases. But she and Tatum are spending half of their time on figuring out how we can improve our operations."

Ava is visibly intrigued. "But who assigns cases and checks quality?"

Jerry grins. "The teams do that. Each of the pods is mapped to a sales region."

Ava shakes her head. "Gee, I wish I could do that. But that would never work with the folks I have."

"I wouldn't be so sure," Jerry replies. "I thought the same thing up until a few months ago. But I've come to realize that if you design the work properly, create good jobs, allow employees to own the work from start to finish, and connect them to the customer, they will step up to the plate."

Ava is clearly skeptical. "What do you mean by 'good jobs'? I think my people have good jobs. We have good salaries, great benefits, and the culture's not bad either."

Jerry shakes his head. "Ava, I'm not talking salary or benefits. I am talking about meaningful work, autonomy, and feedback."

Cameron has been following their back and forth, and now he chimes in. "Jerry, but what does any of that have to do with our Project Sunrise problem?"

Jerry sighs. "Probably not a lot."

Ava is silent for a second and then interjects, "Well, maybe there is something to it. If you don't need supervisors, that could be a massive cost saving. For example, we have eighty people in my group. Well, actually seventy-one, given our turnover. But twelve of them are supervisors."

Cameron pipes in. "That's not so bad, a span of control of seven."

Ava adds, "That is what I thought too, but now I wonder if Jerry is not on to something here."

And then Jerry has a light-bulb moment. "I wonder how Elrod is addressing this issue? He told everyone that he can get lower-cost resources that he can train quickly to do simple tasks. But if you go down that path, then you need an army of supervisors to assign, track, and review the work. Before we made that change, I had three people doing just that, and those were my most experienced—and most expensive—people."

"That makes sense," Ava agrees. "The same is true in my shop. What you just described is exactly what my supervisors are doing."

Now Jerry is on a roll. "So, the real cost of breaking work into tiny tasks is the effort that goes into managing and supervising it. And that's where the savings are!"

Cameron seems a bit confused. "So how exactly does that help us? I mean, unless of course we fire the supervisors?"

Jerry shakes his head. "No, that is not the answer. We redeploy them. But I really wonder whether Elrod included all the supervisors in his numbers."

Ava is still mulling over the supervisor topic. "Hey, Jerry, do you mind explaining a bit more how you went about this whole thing?"

"I would be delighted! How much time do you have?"

Cameron and Ava look at each other, and then Cameron replies, "As much time as you need."

Jerry smiles. "Okay, then." He begins to share everything he learned from Cuthbert. To get started, he asks them to tell him about their best job. Cameron's favorite job was working in construction between high school and college. "We built an entire house from the ground up, start to finish. I still drive past that house every once in a while, whenever I drop my son off at swim class. Still makes me proud."

Ava's favorite job was being a sales rep for a small manufacturer. "The owner gave me a lot of leeway. I did everything, from prospecting to contract negotiations. I owned my territory. Nobody else to blame. It was great in so many ways."

Jerry explains the six different elements of the "good job" framework and the benefit of designing motivating jobs. And then he walks them through how he applied the concept to his onboarding department.

Cameron is impressed. "So that's how you came up with the pod concept? Very interesting."

Ava concurs, thinking out loud, "I wonder whether this could work in Customer Service."

"Why not?" asks Jerry.

"Well, let's see," Ava plays along. "End-to-end responsibility for the work product? We currently don't have that. Everybody is quite specialized, so there are a lot of handoffs between the various teams. Also, variety is pretty low. Purpose . . . hmmm. I hope everybody knows that their work matters. Autonomy? Honestly, very limited. Our tech is lousy. Oh, and what was the last one?"

"Feedback," Jerry replies.

"Okay, that is a part where I think we are doing great. We measure a lot of stuff, and the supervisors listen to a lot of the recorded sessions."

When Jerry explains to her the more potent and self-fulfilling alternatives to simply getting feedback from one's supervisor, Ava sighs. "Okay, so based on those parameters the work is poorly designed. I get your point. So maybe we should start exploring this."

Jerry walks Ava and Cameron through their implementation journey, from assessing the workload to aligning each pod to a sales region, and explains the triple-win concept: high productivity, engaged employees, happy customers.

After Jerry finishes, Cameron looks at Ava. "Well, Ava, what do you think?"

"I have to say, this sounds very interesting. I mean, you know our turnover problem. If this can help with retention, I would certainly give it a try," Ava replies with some optimistic enthusiasm.

Cameron is pleased. "This was a very productive session. Thanks for sharing, Jerry. Let's see what Elrod proposes, but I feel pretty good about our arguments. Thanks, I will see you both on Friday."

On Friday, Jerry's planned 8:00 a.m. call to Cuthbert rings four times and gets dumped into voicemail. He leaves a short message.

Five minutes later Cuthbert calls him back. "Hi, Jerry. Sorry, plane was a bit delayed. Just got off. Greetings from London."

"Please say hello to Charles the Third," Jerry jokes.

Cuthbert laughs. "Hey, Jerry, I am sorry, but I only have a few minutes. How can I help?"

Jerry gives a brief update on Project Sunrise.

"I see," Cuthbert says, "the bean counters are hard at work."

"Exactly. I was wondering if you have any advice as to how we should approach this. I mean, we could argue that our approach requires a lot fewer supervisors and that customers are happier. But do you think that is enough?"

"Well, freeing up the supervisors will definitely save you money. And don't forget about the turnover. Didn't you say turnover in the call center was, like, 100 percent or something?"

"Well actually, a bit more than that."

"Well, if you make the work intrinsically motivating, turnover becomes a nonissue. How long does it take your friend in Customer Service to train people? Let's assume at least six weeks, so with eighty people that translates into ten extra heads. Hey, Jerry, I really need to run, but I think you have a good argument here. Best of luck!"

After the call, Jerry feels a lot less anxious.

SHOWDOWN

L *ike a movie sequel,* Jerry thinks, as they all reassemble in the boardroom. The same cast of characters as last time, plus two new faces in suits. Jerry immediately recognizes them as the two guys he had seen with Elrod in the cafeteria. Now he is certain they are consultants.

Bellamy is nowhere to be seen yet. Then Jerry feels his phone vibrate. A text from Bellamy: "Sorry, bud, can't join today. But the cavalry is on its way. Good luck."

The cavalry?

Elrod walks up to the speaker lectern and pushes a button on his laptop, making the projection screen come to life. "Welcome back, folks. And just a reminder to treat this meeting as strictly confidential; we don't want to create a panic." He moves on to introduce the two new faces at the table. "Meet Jeff Snape and Roger McIntyre from our consulting partner, Peak Solutions. They have helped a lot of companies successfully implement a shared services model."

The suits smile politely. Elrod continues: "Last time, as you may recall, we had a bit of a discussion on the customer experience. In the interim, I asked Jeff and Roger about that, and they assured me that implementing a shared services model does not negatively affect the customer experience. And we ran the numbers again. Richard and his team in Finance updated the model, and as you can see, the financial benefits are even bigger than we initially thought."

Everybody stares at the screen, trying to make sense out of the spreadsheet Elrod is showing. "Up here you see the labor cost comparison. The average pay in Ava's group is $19 an hour for operators. Jerry's team is around $35 an hour. Procurement and HR are right smack in the middle. So, we are using $25 as the average labor cost. Just to keep it simple, we assumed everybody works two thousand hours and a total of one hundred heads. That gets us to an annual labor cost of $5 million, give or take."

Elrod looks around the table before continuing, "Our friends from Peak here are confident that we will get some economies of scale here. We are assuming 20 percent. And we think that we can lower the hourly rate to $17.50. Now that translates into an annual run rate of about $2.8 million, which saves us a whopping $2.2 million each year. Now, we will have some one-off costs in connection with implementing a new workflow management and the consulting support needed, but even with that factored in we should be able to save about $7.4 million over the course of four years." He looks around the room triumphantly.

Cameron raises his hand from the table and interjects, "Elrod, I have a few questions."

He smiles. "How do you think you get 20 percent economies of scale? Ava's group alone is about eighty people. I find it hard to believe that we can save 20 percent if we simply add 20 percent more heads." Before Elrod can respond, he forges on,

"And I still don't understand how you think we can find people to do the job for 30 percent less." He stares at Elrod. "Care to elaborate?"

Elrod glances over to the suits. "Guys, could you chime in? Roger?"

Roger stands up. *Nice suit*, thinks Jerry. *Not cheap.* "Sure thing," Roger begins. "We have done this a lot for other insurance companies. And we found that if we break the work into very specific transactions and use a system to manage the workflow, we can cut back on a lot of training. That in turn allows us to use much less expensive resources."

Before he can carry on, Ava interrupts. "Hey, what kind of turnover did you factor into your model?"

Roger smiles. "We assumed 30 percent."

Ava starts to laugh. "Well, sorry to break this to you, but our call center turnover is running at 125 percent." Everybody turns to her. Ava continues, "So, I don't really understand how you think that will drop to 30 percent. I would imagine that these are fairly crappy jobs. I mean, who can make do on $12 an hour?"

Jerry has been holding back but senses that this is the moment to engage. "Oh, Roger, one more question. How will these less expensive resources be managed?"

Roger seems confused. "What do you mean?"

"Well, Ava here needs one supervisor for every seven operators. And we in onboarding had been operating with one supervisor for every four employees, given the complexity of our workflows—although that was before we redesigned the work. So that suggests to me that we should assume we will need more supervisors to manage the shared services center, no?"

Elrod jumps in. "Well, no, Jerry, we assume we will have a span of control of twenty. So, we will actually need a lot fewer supervisors. The workflow system will tell people what to do."

Cameron looks around the room and states, "Elrod, I think there is a better way. Hey, Jerry, would you be kind enough to explain to the group what you have been working on?"

Great assist, Jerry thinks. He smiles. "With pleasure, Cameron." He quickly glances around the room. "As I said, we used to have a very similar model to what Elrod here is proposing. We broke the work into small tasks, and the supervisors were responsible for assigning the tasks and checking the work. If you factor in the higher salaries of the supervisors, you will realize that managing the work was about 25 percent of our people cost. Actually, a bit higher, if I include myself in that cost. But with the changes we made, we have basically eliminated the supervisor role."

Seeing some confusion in the faces around the table, Jerry clarifies, "We did not lay anybody off, if that is what you are wondering. No. We reinvested those resources into training and process improvement—which will allow us to become even more productive further down the road. We empowered the teams, so they are now managing their own workloads. And guess what? It is so much more effective. Used to take us three months to process a case, and of course we would end up missing the go-live date, which often created a lot of extra work and headaches for Ava and her crew."

Jerry waits a second. Had he lost the audience? He moves to simplify. "So here is the bottom line. We created empowered teams that own each case from start to finish. We are now able to implement a case in a fraction of the time it used to take us. We turned a highly fragmented job where nobody knew what was happening before and after into a job that is actually inter-esting, making the work more purposeful. And I think we can do the same with Ava's group."

Elrod has been holding his tongue, but now he seizes the opportunity. "Well, Jerry, that is very nice, but we are talking money here, dollars and cents. So maybe you want to explain to us how what you are doing helps us save money?"

"Fair point, Elrod. I think we can save a lot of money by put-ting the work back together. We can create real accountability for the work by redesigning the process so that those doing the work own it from start to finish. That should save us at least 15 percent. I also think that it will reduce our turnover. I mean, look at Ava's group. It takes them six weeks to train people, and they stay for less than a year, so that is at least another 10 percent. So that makes 25 percent. So we should be able to save $1.25 million each year, or a total of $5 million. And that does not even factor in the reduction of customer service calls, which we expect to go down significantly."

Elrod grins. "Well, I don't know if we can trust your funny math. Using shared services is a best practice, I am sure you noticed that."

Jerry is not giving up. "But what about the customer experience?"

Elrod grunts. "Well, what about it?"

Having Bellamy in this meeting at this moment would have really helped, Jerry thinks. But just then, there is a knock at the door. Everybody looks up. The door opens, and Shelley walks in, followed by two men in suits Jerry does not recognize. "Sorry for running late," Shelley says, "but we were stuck in traffic. Do you mind if we crash your party?"

Everybody looks perplexed. Gordon gets up. "Shelley, so nice to see you. I imagine Bellamy asked you to fill in for him? Perfect timing, we are just talking about the customer experience."

Shelley smiles. "Gordon, nice to see you again. And hello, everybody." She gestures toward the two men standing near the door. "May I introduce you to George Bain and Jason White?" The two men wave. "George is one of our most prolific brokers. And Jason is the head of HR for Northpoint." She looks at Jerry, grinning. "Bellamy thought it would be good for y'all to talk to actual customers."

The cavalry has arrived indeed! What a smart move! Jerry thinks. The two men step into the room. Jason White looks like the archetypical HR leader: white hair, horn-rimmed spectacles, late fifties. And George looks every bit the part of the hard-driving broker. Lean, hair slicked back, toothy smile. "Thanks for having us," he says as he smiles and takes a seat.

Jason does not. "Which of you is Jerry Crawford?" he asks. When Jerry raises his hand, his eyes light up. "You and your team, you guys are rock stars. Peter has been singing your praises. Pleasure to meet you, son!"

Elrod and his crew seem lost. Gordon on the other hand is excited; he jumps up from his chair and walks over to Jason and George to shake hands with the men. "So nice to meet you," Gordon practically gushes. "We are so delighted to have your business—again."

Elrod realizes the meeting is slipping away from him. "Ahem, nice to have you all join us, but maybe we can move on?"

But Gordon cuts him off. Pointing at Jerry, he looks at George and Jason. "We were just discussing some organizational topics.

202 | FIXING WORK

Jerry told us about the changes he has been making, and we are all very curious as to your perspective."

Jason and George glance at each other. George is the first to respond. "Well, you all know that onboarding is never easy. And yet, it is so crucially important—first impressions and all that. But quite frankly, Cons has been pretty terrible at it. Well, until recently." He looks at Gordon. "I used to get an onslaught of emails from Shelley, which I would then have to channel to the right person at the client. And then I would have to relay the responses back to Shelley. But now," he pauses, "now all of that has stopped. As I understand it, your onboarding folks talk directly to the client—they're getting their information direct from the horse's mouth, if you'll forgive the expression." He smiles at Jason as he says this, who smiles back. George continues, "In fact, now even your bills are accurate for a change." George glances at Jason again. "Care to comment?"

Jason leans forward. "Listen, I was responsible for throwing you guys out the last time you royally messed things up." He looks at Shelley. "Then the new vendor we brought in was just as bad as you guys were. So when Bellamy came with an offer we could not refuse, we decided to give it another try. But, to be perfectly honest, we were bracing ourselves for another rough ride." He looks at Jerry. "But you guys have really changed. My team was blown away by the experience. Peter, my benefits guy, has been singing your praise ever since." Jerry feels more eyeballs on him now.

"So, whatever you are doing here, it works," Jason adds. "I'd hope that you'll keep it up!"

And then Shelley goes in for the kill. "I know you all are trying to save us a few bucks and make us more profitable. But

I don't think you realize how hard it is for us folks in Sales to make it rain if nobody has our back or feels accountable for delivering the case. Jerry, me and my team, we love what you have done." Shelley fixes her gaze on Gordon. "Thanks for your support, Gordon." She looks at Jason and George. "Gentlemen, thanks for making the trip and dropping in. We have a lunch reservation at one. Should we be going?"

After the door closes, the mood in the room has changed. The two consultants know it, and they start to look at their phones. Elrod is trying to refocus the team on the presentation but knows he has lost. Gordon looks at Elrod, then Ben, and then Richard, his CFO. "Well, that was very enlightening. Elrod, thank you for the presentation. But from where I sit, it seems that what Jerry has been doing is working. I don't want to jeopardize that."

Gordon then looks at Cameron and Ava. "And you guys are implementing the same idea in Customer Service? Can't wait to see how that works out."

Cameron nods enthusiastically. "Yes, Gordon, we are going full steam ahead."

Jerry suppresses a smile. Gordon surveys the room with serious eyes to command attention and then pronounces, "Look everyone, I like saving money as much as the next guy—maybe *more* than the next guy." Now Gordon's gaze is squarely on Elrod as he continues, "But I am a bit concerned about the implications of your proposal, Elrod."

Elrod is visibly uncomfortable. Is that sweat beading on his forehead?

And then Gordon drives a stake through the heart. "I think we pass. I mean, I know it is a leap of faith, but the sales guys love it, the brokers love it, the customers love it. And when you come right down to it, when you get past the dollars and cents, we are still in a people business." Gordon looks around the room for any dissent from his execs. Seeing none he adds, "So maybe we can find those savings somewhere else?"

Elrod looks defeated.

"Ben," Gordon instructs, "I say we look at this again in a year. Oh, and Cameron?"

"Yes?"

"You better take Jerry and his team out for a nice meal. Okay, meeting adjourned!"

As Jerry walks out, he feels a tap on his shoulder. He turns around. Gordon. "Jerry, I will ask my assistant to set up a meeting for us later. Okay?"

Jerry grins. "Of course, Gordon, anytime!"

As he steps into the hallway, Jerry sees Elrod huddling with the suits near the elevators. They are probably disappointed that the meeting did not go as they had expected. Well, not his problem.

As Jerry walks briskly back to his office, his phone rings. It's Bellamy.

"Jerry here."

"How did the cavalry do?"

Jerry laughs. "Very well. I was just about out of bullets when they showed up."

He hears Bellamy chuckle. "Well, I figured they should hear it from the horse's mouth. Sorry I missed the show, but I assume Shelley did all right?"

"More than all right!"

"Happy to hear. Hey, let's catch up soon. Bye, Jerry."

FULL SPEED AHEAD

The first thing Jerry does as he gets to the office is to grab Mary and Johnny. "Let's catch up." They quietly commandeer the small conference room, and as soon as the door is closed, Jerry gives them the play-by-play.

"So, the shared services idea is dead?" Johnny asks, when Jerry finishes, wanting to be absolutely sure.

"Yes, indeed."

They are both visibly relieved. "Full speed ahead?" Mary asks.

Jerry laughs. "Yes, indeed," he repeats. "But I think we need to expand our reach." He explains that Ava is thinking about adopting some of the same ideas and techniques. "I was wondering if the two of you could help her get started?"

Johnny grins. "My pleasure, Jerry!"

After that, he calls Bob from HR. "Hey, how much flexibility do we have when it comes to our compensation budget?"

Bob seems confused. "What do you mean?"

"Well, I am thinking about using the money we set aside for the open supervisor role, Julia's replacement. I'd like to give everybody an across-the-board raise instead."

There is a long silence. "Well, Jerry, that is a bit unusual. But I guess we could make that happen. Are you certain?"

Jerry laughs. "Yes, Bob, I am sure. We are asking the team to really take some ownership and responsibility, and I think they should be fairly compensated."

Bob laughs. "Okay, I get it. Consider it done. I will have to get approval for that, of course."

"Of course. Thanks, Bob!" Jerry hangs up.

Jerry then calls Ava and lets her know that Johnny and Mary are on standby. Ava seems very grateful and even eager to get started.

And then Jerry calls Cuthbert. When the voicemail comes on, he leaves a short message: "Hey, Mike. Jerry here. Just wanted to let you know the second round went well. Couldn't have done it without you!"

He sits in during two pod meetings, but his mind is elsewhere, so he decides to call it a day.

Haley is clearly surprised when he walks in the door at 4:30 p.m. "Howdy, stranger, how was your week?"

Jerry smiles. "Fabulous, darling, absolutely fabulous."

PATHS FORWARD

A little party never hurt nobody, Jerry thinks, as he finishes up preparations for the barbecue he's hosting. He has invited his entire team, plus Cameron and Ava, to celebrate what they have achieved so far.

Jerry thinks back to his conversation with Gordon four weeks earlier. He had been surprised when Gordon had offered him Cameron's role. He had been uncomfortable at first, but after Gordon explained that Cameron had submitted his resignation, he had felt less awkward about it. Nevertheless, before he had accepted the offer, he made sure Gordon agreed with one condition—that he could continue the work design journey. Gordon had assured him that the main reason he was selected for the promotion was their hope that Jerry would work the same magic for the rest of Client Services.

When, in that same conversation, Gordon had asked Jerry who should be the next leader of the onboarding team, he had struggled for a few seconds, before ultimately recommending Mary. Her focus on getting things done was what the department now needed most. And while he had felt bad for Johnny at the time, Jerry now has more confidence than ever before that greater opportunities with the company will come. Johnny will have his day, too.

Jerry and Gordon had agreed to wait with the announcement until Cameron's last day, which is this coming Monday.

Speaking of the devil, he sees Cameron approaching the grill. He seems happy. They chat for a few minutes. Mr. Sunny-Side Up is excited about his new role, the senior vice president of operations for a property insurer. Good for him.

The onboarding crew is all here, appreciative of the substantial raise they received when Jerry repurposed the money set aside for Julia's replacement.

Mary walks up to him, greeting him with a cheery, "Hey, boss."

Jerry chuckles.

Mary being Mary, she cannot resist giving him an update on the team's performance. "Jerry, we are down to eighty cases. Oh, and Roheela? She is a rock star."

Jerry smiles. "So, you think she can fill your big shoes?"

Mary laughs. "Actually, yes. I look forward to helping our Customer Service friends." She has a big grin on her face. Did she know he was taking over Cameron's job—and that she would be offered his? Had she already accepted?

Haley is calling him. "Jerry, there is someone at the door for you."

When he makes his way to the front door, he is surprised to see Bellamy. "What a nice surprise. Come on in!" he exclaims.

But Bellamy shakes his head. "Sorry, Jerry, I'm double-booked. But I wanted to drop this off." He points to the four boxes of doughnuts next to the doorbell. Then he winks at Jerry, "Oh, and congrats on the promotion—well deserved! Keep it going!!"

How did he know?

EPILOGUE

Time flies when you are having fun. It has been nearly two years, Jerry realizes, since he serendipitously ran into Mike Cuthbert at that little bakery. And that chance encounter launched him on a quest to fix work—first with the onboarding team, then with Customer Service, and now maybe with the whole company.

When in their final one-on-one meeting before the year-end break Gordon asks whether he would be open to a new role, Jerry is suspicious at first. It has been only a year since he took over Cameron's job. And yes, they had begun making great strides, Jerry acknowledges, but there is so much more to do, he tells Gordon. The onboarding group has continued its journey, actually moving beyond pods—now every single member of the department is able to handle any case, from start to finish. But Ava's Customer Service team still has a ways to go.

Yet Gordon is persistent. "Yes, Jerry, there is still plenty to do, but I need you—the company needs you. You have done an amazing job. Just look at this year's engagement numbers." Jerry has to suppress a smile; he is well aware that Client Services has recently scored off the charts on the various engagement metrics.

"Jerry, you started something here that we can take further—that we must take further. If we can get everybody in the organization to be as engaged as your folks, we will be unbeatable. No doubt. So I need you to do your magic across the entire company."

Nobody becomes a CEO unless they are a good salesperson first, Jerry thinks. He asks Gordon for a few days to think it over.

Gordon is right, Jerry later reasons as he makes his way home.

If they are able to activate only a fraction of the onboarding team's energy, they will be unbeatable. But he also worries a bit. Applying what Cuthbert had taught him in his own department had been challenging at times, and Jerry realizes that in this new role, he would have to get his peers to buy in to his ideas. *Influence without authority. Great!*

But then again, an opportunity to change an entire company as head of transformation? That could be fun.

ACKNOWLEDGMENTS

This book would not exist had John Uzzi not introduced Thomas, all the way back in 2004, to the work design framework described in the book. And John was instrumental in updating the framework—which builds on the work of Douglas McGregor, Frederick Herzberg, Richard Hackman, and Greg Oldham—for the modern era. We also acknowledge Dart Lindsley, who deserves credit for looking at work as a product and employees as customers of the work product.

Thomas also thanks his clients, who have allowed him for the last twenty-five years to work on their pressing issues and to learn from them; his team at Purpose Works; and his former colleagues at Rath & Strong, Valeocon, and OXYGY. David acknowledges and thanks Ellie Frolic, as well as his many amazing colleagues and friends throughout the years.

Appendix

JERRY'S NOTES

BENEFITS OF WORK DESIGN:

- Engaged and motivated employees

- Satisfied customers

- Improved productivity

THE INGREDIENTS OF A GOOD JOB:

- *Purpose:* The outcome is very important to others.

- *Entirety:* An employee is responsible for the entire work product.

- *Variety:* An employee is able to apply a broad range of skills.

- *Autonomy:* An employee has the ability to use judgment and discretion.

- *Feedback:* Doing the work provides feedback.

- *Tech:* The technology used is fit for purpose.

THE JOB DESIGN SURVEY:

- I have almost complete responsibility for deciding how and when the work is to be done.

- Just doing the work provides me with opportunities to figure out how well I am doing.

- I do a complete task from start to finish. The results of my efforts are clearly visible and identifiable.

- I have the opportunity to do a number of different tasks, using a wide variety of skills and talents.

- What I do affects others in very important ways.

- The technology I use to perform my work is well designed and makes the job easier.

HOW TO CREATE INTRINSICALLY MOTIVATING WORK:

1. Minimize non-mission-critical, low-value-added work.

2. Consolidate tasks and create whole jobs.

3. Simplify coordination and minimize distractions.

4. Create mission ownership.

5. Establish direct customer relationships.

6. Open feedback channels.

7. Delegate responsibility to the lowest level.

THREE ELEMENTS OF DRIVING CHANGE:

1. Communicate

2. Engage

3. Educate

IS MOTIVATIONAL WORK DESIGN RIGHT FOR YOU?

If you think that motivational work design could benefit your organization, consider whether the following statements apply to your organization:

- We could be more effective.

- We struggle to become more agile and adaptable.

- Our current work processes are highly fragmented.

- We struggle to retain top talent and deal with increased turnover.

- We are concerned about employee engagement.

- Employees lack authority to resolve issues or improve workflows.

- It is difficult to determine accountability when issues arise.

- Employees are unclear about what outcomes they own.

- We need to improve the customer experience.

If you agree with more than five of these statements and you believe that most employees want to do a good job, seek responsibility, and can be self-directed, then you should explore how redesigning work to be intrinsically motivating could help your business.

———————

For easy next steps to fix work in your organization, go to www.fixing-work.com. Learn more about motivational work design, check out our free work design diagnostic tool and other free resources, and join a growing community of leaders looking to make work more productive, valuable, meaningful, and impactful.

ABOUT THE AUTHORS

DAVID HENKIN is an accomplished executive and entrepreneur with a proven record of success in prominent global companies as well as start-ups. The author of several books, he has taught in a top-rated university business school program while also serving as a consultant and executive coach for corporate and nonprofit leaders. David is based in Philadelphia and holds an MBA from Villanova University, an MA from the City College of New York, and a BS from the University of Maryland.

THOMAS BERTELS is the president and founder of Purpose Works, a management consulting firm on a mission to make work more productive, valuable, meaningful, and impactful. He has twenty-five years of experience working with companies ranging from Fortune 10 firms to start-ups to improve organizational effectiveness and transform how work gets done. He has published several books and countless articles. Thomas is based in New Jersey and holds an MBA from the Stern School of Business.